TH
FORTUNATE
HILLS

THE HISTORY OF THE CHILTERN SOCIETY
1965 - 2001

Howard Gilbert

The **Chiltern**
Society

We care for the Chilterns

Published by The Chiltern Society
registered charity number 1085163

*A company limited by guarantee registered in
England and Wales number 4138448*

We care for the Chilterns

The Chiltern Society continues to do the work envisaged at its foundation in 1965, and expanded as needed and possible to meet new demands and pressures.
This work - incorporating much fun and good times too - is aimed at helping to keep the Greater Chilterns area a good place in which to live and work, and visit.
Anyone can join the Society who would wish to support the aims, and the means of achieving those aims. Offers of help are welcomed, but those who feel they can only help by paying a subscription are every bit as welcome.

All enquiries should be addressed to:
The Chiltern Society Office, White Hill Centre,
White Hill, Chesham,
Bucks HP5 1AG
Telephone: 01494 771250
Fax: 01494 793745
e-mail: office@chilternsociety.org.uk
visit the website at www.chilternsociety.org.uk

COVER *Offley Holes, Preston, Bedfordshire*

This book is an example of the successful mix of voluntary efforts of Howard Gilbert and Cic Upcott, who both spent many hours preparing the text and finding pictures, helping Louise Kirby in her professional capacity preparing the work for the printer. Many thanks to them for their dedication.

Photography by many members, from early days to recent years - as many are unknown, please accept our grateful thanks to you all, though unnamed.

ISBN 0 904148-09-2

Designed and typeset by Louise Kirby
Printed in Great Britain by Unwin Brothers Limited,
The Gresham Press, Old Woking, Surrey GU22 9LH

CONTENTS

FOREWORD

For so many of us, who are fortunate enough to live or work in, or visit the Chilterns, they remain very special to us personally. But they are also important nationally as well as being particularly important in the South East of Britain, given their closeness to London and the Thames Valley.

Thankfully they remain still, as Hepple and Doggett have said in their wonderful book *The Chilterns*, somewhere with 'a sense of place'.

But there is a great human story behind how the area has, in recent years, managed to retain that special feeling. Undoubtedly the designation of the Chilterns as an AONB (Area of Outstanding Natural Beauty) was most important, and that of itself was a major early triumph for the founder members of the Chiltern Society. But since then the Chilterns have without doubt been *The Fortunate Hills* because they have had such a wonderfully diverse group of people caring for them in such a variety of ways: The Chiltern Society.

This book is a story of how something, which started with two people determined to care for what was precious to them, has now grown to 7500 caring people. Above all it is a practical book because the Chiltern Society is above all a practical organisation, run by practical people voluntarily carrying out between them thousands of practical tasks each year to look after the environment they care for. This has required leadership which in turn has produced a professionalism admired and respected by many, and I would like to pay my own personal tribute to the many people personally highlighted in this book by Howard Gilbert.

Most importantly I think Howard has stressed the importance of the people involved in creating what is now known as 'the eyes and ears' of the Chilterns. This makes it a fascinating book for anyone interested in effective human endeavour as well as anyone caring for the environment around us. This is a great example of what can be achieved if you believe in it, find others who share your aims, do your homework carefully and communicate well.

Congratulations and thanks to Howard for writing a book of such interest and significance to many, whether or not they yet know *The Fortunate Hills*.

Robin Rowland Chairman, 2002 -

INTRODUCTION

This book is about the history of the Chiltern Society, from its foundation on 8 May 1965. One hundred people who shared Christopher Hall and Ted Castle's concern for the conservation of the Chiltern Hills witnessed the occasion. The story concludes in June 2001 when, with a membership of over 7,500, under Michael Rush's imaginative Chairmanship, the Society became a company limited by guarantee. By so doing it had set its sights firmly towards the new century and renewed the purpose of those founding pioneers.

In October 2000, the Annual Report recorded the Strategic Planning Team Report proposing the Society's future charted course:

Our Vision for the Chilterns in the 21st Century and
Our Vision for the Society for the next Ten Years.

This Report reviewed achievable strategic developments, re-affirmed a number of existing plans and policies, and recommended areas for action. By the end of the new century the Society aimed to be an even more lively, vigorous organisation working to care for the Chilterns.

Three earlier histories have been published, documenting the Society's progress to 1992. They are: 65-75, The Chiltern Society's *First Ten Years; Seventy Five to Eighty One, the Next Six Years; The Eleven Years 1982-1992*. This new book melds these three together, presenting the salient points of each but adding some dimensions that the earlier writers did not include. Part Four covers the years from around 1993 to approximately 2001/02 and describes many of the events, the endeavours, the successes and the anxieties of that period.

Michael Rush commissioned this history; his helpful initial observations and enthusiasm were very encouraging. The extent of his involvement and leadership in developing the Society since he became Vice-Chairman in October 1995, and Chairman from October 1997, emerged gradually as the book progressed. Much detail is included about the achievements during his time as Chairman. The extent and depth of his commitment is striking, for he spared no effort in engaging in every Society activity. Because of its chronological closeness to the time when this book is written, I have preferred to use this introduction to focus the record. My successor will be better able to place it historically; nevertheless it is right here to pay tribute to a significantly successful period in the Society's growth, and the work of its motivating Chairman, Michael Rush.

Between 1995 and 1997 Michael continued the campaign for re-watering the River Misbourne, a cause in which he strongly supported the endeavours of Vic Wotton. He accompanied Barry Scott (then Chairman) on a study tour of southern AONBs, concluding it with a detailed comparative analysis and assessment showing that the Chilterns AONB was substantially under-resourced. He organised the 30th Anniversary celebrations in fine style to the joy and pleasure of 250 Society members. On becoming Chairman In 1997 he immediately focused the Society's attention upon the need for change and development, particularly the importance of close cooperation with the Chiltern Conference, soon to become the shadow Chilterns Conservation Board.

During the next five years, five major achievements stand to Michael's credit, together with many others where personal attention and commitment facilitated direction and purpose. The Awards to the Mobile Shop team are an example, among many. Primacy must go to the initiation of the Strategic Review chaired by Robin Rowland, which produced the twin visions of the future for the Society, and 80 practical, reasoned recommendations for the way forward. Secondly, the persuasion of the Executive Council to support the public appeal for funds, under the patronage of Jeremy Irons, to purchase Ewelme Watercress Beds. Thirdly, the encouragement and backing given to the Rights of Way Millennium Project, the Chiltern Way. Fourth, his promotion of the ultimately successful appeal, which enabled the Woodland Trust's purchase of the ancient Penn Wood. Fifth, the review of the Society's procedural and administrative functioning that has improved Executive Council processes, and set up a well-equipped administrative Office in Chesham.

The record of all this, and much other activity, will be found in the pages of Part Four; Michael's commitment and care for the Society has been affirmed by many members, strongly endorsing a view formed during my own reading and preparation. Two simple examples stand for many more: he encouraged Sue and Paul Thomas to establish the Cycle group, he and Linda, his wife, joining the first organised ride. The other is the very full detailed response to Cic Upcott's history information request that I have used in writing the last phases of the Misbourne story. Members have told me about numerous similar instances of his close interest, encouragement and involvement. His Chairmanship was a time of substantial advance in many areas of the Society's work.

The change to a larger and more comprehensive volume, from the originally envisaged amalgamation plus the last 12 years or so in a fourth volume, was made by me following the responses received to Cic Upcott's letter in 2001 to all those likely to contribute. Because of the number and size of those contributions, and the additional information that could be included - and the fact that June 2001 brought the first era to an end - it seemed useful to offer a fuller account of the 36 years of growth incorporating the earlier records.

The substance of those generous answers to Cic's letter have informed, infused, and focused much of the text in Part Four. Facts, figures, and helpful information abounded; personal views of particular occasions were valued and are acknowledged wherever possible. I am particularly appreciative of permission to quote given by a number of those who sent in material, and to all who answered, whether quoted or not, their views and remembrances are ever present in the text. Without the insight that all these contributions have brought, much would have been left out.

Many active, experienced and senior members of the Society have helpfully reviewed drafts, answered telephoned queries, and returned scripts with generous observations and constructive suggestions. My gratitude in all of this goes to Christopher Barry, Rob Bethell, Christine Breden, Don Brooks, Ray Challinor, Peter Cleasby, John Coombe, Francis Cory-Wright, Roy Crisp, Dave Howarth, Walter Horn, Beryl Hunt, Norman Joyce, Geoffrey Legge, Derek Martin, the late Don Millar, Christopher Morris, John Morris, Edward Newmark, John Norris, Guy Patterson, Christine Preston, John Taylor, Alan Ross, John Rowe, Derek Upcott, Ray Wainwright, Barbara Wallis, and Christopher Wallis.

Almost last in this list of Society members who have given generous help, but not by any means least, I offer an appreciative thanks to Cic Upcott, Publications Editor, who has provided much information, background material, advice, suggestions, comments and text-editing which have enabled the work to reach its final stage; I have much appreciated her support. Also to Christine Preston and her colleagues at the White Hill Centre office for their help in locating important parts of the records they hold, my gratitude for their generous assistance. Finally to Robin Rowland, Chairman from November 2002, who has read the draft and emailed his appreciation, my thanks to him for his enthusiasm, encouragement and interest in the project as he charts the way forward for the Chiltern Society in the first part of this new century.

People from the Chiltern Open Air Museum, and the Chiltern Woodlands Project, both independent incorporated partners of the Society, also have commented helpfully. My gratitude is to Patricia Lindsey, Melissa Maynard and their colleagues at COAM, and John Morris, manager of CWP Ltd. Among many others who have assisted me a particular grateful word must be given to the staff at the Centre for Buckinghamshire Studies, to Leida Smith, Media Officer of Dacorum Borough Council, the Reference Librarians at Herts Dacorum Library, the Hertfordshire branch of the CPRE, and the Archives of the Ministry of Defence: their help has been invaluable.

My special thanks and appreciation of help go to Barbara French, my professional colleague from Mid-Life Options, who has generously read sketches, text drafts and the final copy, offering both constructive comment, and clarification where ambiguity, awkward syntax, and disparate phraseology were apparent. I gratefully acknowledge the help given by Rosemary Harrap of the same consultancy. She is a specialist in script presentation and university MS, and assisted me in the early stages, prior to corrective sight operations. Without either of these colleagues, this final stage could not and would not have been reached.

I hope all members of the Society will enjoy the work as much as I have in its preparation; if errors remain in the text, they are mine.

Howard Gilbert,
Leverstock Green, Herts. October 2003

PART ONE

THE BACKGROUND FOR ACTION IN 1965

The Chiltern Society is a regional charitable organisation managed and run by volunteers, and administered from an office in Chesham. It was founded in 1965 as the outcome of initiatives taken by two journalists, Ted Castle (later a Life Peer) and Christopher Hall, later Secretary of the Ramblers' Association, one-time Director of the Council for the Protection of Rural England (CPRE), and Editor of *The Countryman* magazine.

The catalyst for action was the conjunction of three major threats to the quality of the Chiltern landscape: industrial extension and pollution, motorway development and the loss of many footpaths in the post-war years. Public disquiet and protest, distress and anger, combined to form a body of significant local concern for the future of this beautiful part of southern Britain. An extra, ironic dimension was that much of the immediately local despoliation was being caused by the actions of a Government ministry and its contractors.

Eight years earlier the National Parks Authority had designated 320 square miles of the Chilterns an Area of Outstanding Natural Beauty (AONB). The designation awaited Ministerial approval, but hopes were high and expectations great. The area was one of 33 AONBs nationwide, and joined with the similar determining of national parks during the same decade.

It was early on decided that the Chiltern Society area be over twice this, surrounding the AONB on all sides, reaching into South Bedfordshire and northern Hertfordshire, encompassing Hitchin, and following the line to the Thames bounding South Oxfordshire. The escarpment is the natural northern boundary of the Society area; however, parish boundaries are used as the main definition.

A proposed extension of the opencast quarrying at the Tunnel Cement Works, at Pitstone, below the Ridgeway Path, caused much alarm among the residents of the nearby villages. (The issue, and the consequences of the works operation became one of Society's major commitments for many years ahead.) Cement was in much demand for the New Towns, three of which - Hatfield, Hemel Hempstead and Stevenage – were being built in the area. In addition, as the early Society proceedings record, the prospect of a new city in north Buckinghamshire added to the concerns about the Works extension.

Cement is necessary also for road construction. Britain's first Motorway, opened in the 1950s by Ernest Marples (Minister for Transport), had been carved through the northeast Chilterns. By the mid-60s there was talk of a third lane from Watford to Hemel Hempstead with its implication for traffic growth. Elsewhere, for the residents of Stokenchurch and all who enjoyed Christmas Common and the Wormsley Valley, the steady approach of the second London to Birmingham Motorway (M40) was a matter of much agitated feeling. There was wide-scale felling of beechwoods, replaced by characterless conifers. The projected route (and that finally built) cut through the northern escarpment at its most majestic point overlooking the Oxfordshire Plain. The Pitstone quarries, the new town developments and the Wormsley Valley were conjoint causes for local protest and action.

There were several other reasons for local anxiety of which rights of way were a major and controversial issue. Rapid action seemed necessary, by survey and clearance, contact with local authorities and landowners, together with a systematic clearance work programme for the path network. This was deemed the essential minimum action necessary to restore lost rights of access and passage, together with the necessary signage still not re-erected after World War Two.

These uncertainties and disturbances were matched on a larger, more anxiously frightening scale in national and international politics. The Suez crisis of 1956/57, and the explosion of the British H-bomb were followed by the Cuban missile confrontation between USA and Russia in 1962. The national economy was affected by policies of 'stop-go' regulation, pay pauses, and industrial unrest. An easing of constraints, during which the Prime Minister was reported as saying that the people 'never had it so good', succeeded these. There was also a new growing sense that personal lives were better.

A revolution in life styles: the mid-50s onwards

Significant social change was generated for part of the population through improving family incomes; easier bank credit, relatively low interest rates were readily available with hire purchase facilities.

The home improvement industry (do-it-yourself) began to boom; wider car ownership became possible, leisure and outdoor pursuit opportunities multiplied, the cinema declined rapidly with the arrival of colour television, and the pattern of social life altered. More new houses were built in addition to the developing new towns and the city of Milton Keynes. New and second-hand cars occupied road space in increasing numbers – moving and parked.

Residents in the Chilterns and elsewhere became aware of other developments with positive and negative implications for the quality of life. The farming industry, always close to the small and medium sized towns (Amersham, Berkhamsted, Tring, Chesham, St Albans, Dunstable, Hitchin and Totternhoe, the expanding township around Chinnor Village, Thame and Watlington) was responding to the food demands that new life styles were setting. The production of vegetables, fruit, cereals, and livestock was doubled and doubled again. The countryside altered as hedgerows and trees within them were grubbed out to create larger field enclosures; Dutch elm disease further diminished the tree-scape. Chemical fertilisers replaced organic supply. The number of animals per pasture acre increased greatly, 'agri-business' replaced (or displaced) traditional husbandry as food production rose.

A further change, of which Chiltern people gradually became aware, also affected the

countryside and its uses. Prosperity brought new and enhanced outdoor pursuits; to traditional rambling could be added long distance and hill walking, orienteering, and the first signs of
Ridgeway biking. Many more people were able to afford caravans, frame tents, horse riding,
hang gliding and hot air ballooning. In other AONBs and national parks, rock and mountain
climbing, sailing and canoeing became popular pastimes for young and middle-aged alike. In
the south-west corner of the Chilterns, the Thames attracted small river craft; in the middle
Hills, British Waterways fostered, stimulated and encouraged canal boating in addition to
small motorised launches. Encouraged by Bernard Banfield, the Chiltern Society gave support
in principle to the restoration of the Grand Union Canal's Wendover Arm. In moving from the
post-war 'Fasting Fifties' into the 'Swinging Sixties' and beyond, the British experienced a revolution in living styles and leisure, and some revelled in the apparent prosperity that was
engendered. To the countryside overall, these activities brought a renewal of economic life:
tourism benefited, homes were improved, living standards rose and farming became a more
secure way of life, providing for some a substantial income. The countryside was beginning to
be enjoyed, appreciated and used by more people than ever before.

The effect on the countryside

There was a flip side to this Golden Age, this Leisure Society of the 1960s, one that still
involves the Chiltern Society of today in similar action: to prevent rubbish dumping in the
countryside. A major problem then with the footpaths and isolated corners of the countryside
was that quantities of unwanted household goods, builders' rubbish and even old cars, were
being dumped in them, preventing access. A headline in an early edition of *Chiltern News*
(Autumn 1968) reads "Twenty-two old bicycles" and the article describes their removal (and
a car chassis and body), unwanted and rusting, from woodlands near Tring. One of the first
Society's Anti-Litter groups did the job supported by the local Council, and many more clearance parties were held. Places like the Bledlow and Whiteleaf Crosses were sadly abused, as
local authorities had not yet been able to provide facilities for waste control and re-cycling on
the scale that seemed to be essential. It was a nation-wide issue that the media termed the
'Effluent Society'.

The introduction of intensive farming and agri-business often brought in tandem the blocking or ploughing up of these public rights of way. Landowners sought to limit access, to have
paths diverted or extinguished in order to regulate more closely popular movement over land.
Many of these rights had existed for centuries but now were being deliberately obstructed by
these modern methods of farming and husbandry. Paths, fallen into disuse by lack of signage
after the war, had become overgrown as well as filled with rubbish as a consequence, and
enthusiastic walkers found their movement on legitimate routes often halted by this condition,
or as the result of deliberate blocking and constriction.

The issue of rights of way was uppermost in the minds of the two initiators of the inaugural meeting. It was among the very first activities to be tackled after the Society's formation, and continues today one of its major commitments.

How did it happen? Where exactly did it begin? What were its founders' objectives?

Origins and action

Ted Castle and Christopher Hall were colleagues on the staff of the *Daily Herald*. The Castles lived at Ibstone, and Christopher Hall was a resident of Christmas Common. Both men lunched at the **Cross Keys Tavern** in Covent Garden, close to the *Herald's* offices. Both shared the experience of living and walking in the Chilterns, and talking about this each realised that they shared the sense that the quality of the life and countryside around them was deteriorating, with the growing pressures on the environment and landscape.

Their first thoughts about creating a caring organisation in the Chilterns are recorded by Christopher Hall in 65-75, *The Chiltern Society's first ten years*, published in 1975.

"Ted and I were discussing, as we sometimes did, our common concerns about the Chiltern countryside…We were worried about how the M40 motorway was to be routed across the escarpment west of Stokenchurch; we both grieved at the savage felling of beechwoods and their too frequent replacement with conifers. We were both regular walkers in the area and consequently disgusted by the ploughing and obstruction of many public paths.

Ted said, "We ought to have a society to preserve the Chilterns.

"Easy to say. There were already many village and civic societies, though nothing like the legion of today [1975]. There were also the county branches of the Council for the Preservation (now Protection) of Rural England."

During subsequent lunchtime discussions, the two men decided there was a case for a new society, a caring organisation; letters were sent to everyone in *Who's Who* listing an address in the Chilterns, inviting them to help form a 'society to protect the character and beauty of the Chilterns'; the action was supported by a complementary series of letters to the local and regional Press. A meeting was fixed for Saturday, 8 May 1965 in the Guildhall, High Wycombe.

"Just over 100 people came … and under Ted's Chairmanship agreed, with only one dissentient, … to form the Chiltern Society, an organisation that would command loyalty.

"Before the meeting we had asked Viscount Esher if he would serve as President should the Society be formed. He was an ideal choice. … (A) distinguished architect and conservationist, (living) in the family home, Watlington Park. He had been a Liberal candidate for the local constituency in 1945. He was Chairman of the Oxfordshire Branch of the CPRE…"

Viscount Esher responded helpfully and became the President soon after the Society's formation. He was to serve the Society at this most supportive level for the next 17 years (1965-1982) and a further three(1987-1990), thereafter becoming a Vice-President.

FOUNDERS AND PIONEERS

At the meeting there were others destined to serve and support the fledgling organisation for many years to come, each providing the strong, dedicated and powerful contributions to the work that the Society needed to carry out, and continues still to do. These included Arnold Baines, Chesham Councillor and Chiltern and town historian, later to serve as Chairman and to add substantial research studies to the knowledge of Anglo-Saxon and Romano-British culture in the Chilterns; Bernard Banfield from Pitstone, champion of the cause to limit and control the spread of the cement works that threatened to totally desecrate the landscape around his village and neighbouring Ivinghoe. Later, Bernard became Chairman of the Water Resources Group, maintaining an active interest in the Society until his death in 2001. Jeffrey Hawkins was present at the meeting; he came also from Pitstone where his family had farmed at Pitstone Green for 200 years. He was elected Vice Chairman, serving until 1974, and was a leading founder member of the Historic Works & Building Group (HWBG) that he subsequently chaired. Jeff's father had given the Pitstone Windmill – one of the oldest in Britain dating from c1627 – to the National Trust. Jeff and Christopher Wallis led the team of volunteers who worked on the restoration of the Lacey Green Windmill for the Society between 1967 and 1986, assisted by John Caisley, David Empringham and many others. Jeff Hawkins continued to serve the Society until he died in 2001.

Christopher Morris and Christopher Barry were among the first founders of the Society. Christopher Morris, a civil engineer, became Treasurer in 1966, then Vice Chairman, and Chairman twice in 1969-73 and 1977-81. He was then elected a Vice President in 1985. Writing about him in 1975, Christopher Hall said, "(his) contribution to the Society has been the most distinguished effort of all."

Christopher Barry, a BBC television producer, living in Stokenchurch and vastly aware of the contractorial vandalism accompanying the approaching M40, succeeded Christopher Hall as General Secretary in 1968. He submitted evidence to the Public Inquiries concerning the motorway and was a strong supporter of the Arup-Jellicoe line through the escarpment that the Society, and many other bodies, considered far superior to that which was eventually built. Another founder and pioneer was John Willson, from Downley, High Wycombe, who brought with him the 'town perspective', and became the second Field Officer. Later still he was appointed Planning Adviser, serving until 1979, and worked to bring local town and village amenity societies into the planning fold, since many concerns were shared.

Peter Mould succeeded Christopher Barry as General Secretary from 1971 to 1974. He and Don Gresswell were among what has been described as the 'angry group'; Peter subsequently moved to Wales, but before his departure he provided a nine-point challenge to the membership about the way forward in the future. This was published in *65-75 – the first ten years*. Don Gresswell, having developed the Anti-Litter Group so successfully, helped set up its successor, the ROWG as it still is today, wrote the constitution for them and sought a 'declaration of independence' at the Council Meeting in 1967, which failed.

This strengthened the Society despite the fact that the opposite could have occurred; the principle of specialist autonomous activist groups was established and has continued unchanged ever since. At the time it enabled rapid action on improving the footpath network on which Ted Castle and Christopher Hall had ruminated during their discussions at the Cross Keys Tavern, Covent Garden in 1964.

Eric Schmidt of the founding group became Chairman following the resignation of Ted Castle, early in 1967. He was a marketing director with the Uni-Royal Group, and took a considerable interest in the Historic Works and Buildings Group (HW&BG) activity launched and chaired by Christopher Barry. "He was one of the best chairmen an honorary secretary could ever hope to work with", said Christopher Hall, who described him as giving firm guidance. The record calls him a "hard-driving Chairman" determined to achieve results as efficiently as possible; both he and his wife were devoted to community work,she is a member of the womens' Institute.

First Field Officer – policy in the making

Jean Buchanan created the job of Field Officer and, as Christopher Hall recorded, "travelled many hundreds of miles each month". As general planning issues came to the Executive Committee she took them on and investigated those that clearly required on-the-spot attention. She consulted local opinion, planners and developers, and her work undoubtedly focused the direction that the Society's activities took during those early years. Her reports to the Council and Executive deal with immediate issues such as road construction, environmental vandalism, concern for historic buildings and the AONB heritage. She carried forward the policy that the Society continues to follow today: to work with the grain of issues, only engaging in confrontation where there is intransigence, and obstructive bureaucracy or obscurantist attitudes.

Writing in 1975, Peter Mould says:

"Thus today, cooperation and participation are more frequent themes than confrontation in dealings with, for example, planners and farmers.

Peter adds that this form of approach was more effective and in part due to an "amenity group whose opinions are respected on account of our membership and expertise". "There is", he writes, "a (growing) general trend towards participation between government and governed, and greater public acceptance (and in official circles) of the 'need to preserve and enhance the quality of life'. People respond more to persuasion, yet 'we' will not be inhibited if confrontation is necessary."

Bernard Banfield, Arnold Baines, the Christophers: Barry, Hall, Morris and Wallis, Jean Buchanan, Jeffrey Hawkins, Peter Mould, Eric Schmidt, Don Gresswell, and John Willson were among the pioneers who drove the Society forward from the foundation day in May 1965.

Viscount Esher was in strong support for the first 30 years as President and President Emeritus, and contributed much to the discussions and delegations who, from time to time, visited Ministers, lobbied Parliament and other authorities.

What was it about the Chiltern landscape that sustained their early enthusiasm and, for several of the founders' group, kept them committed and involved throughout the rest of their lives? Why today, in 2003, does that sustaining interest attract a membership (corporate, family, and individual) exceeding 7500? What in essence are the Chilterns? What makes the area so special?

THE CHILTERNS – WHY SO SPECIAL?

"In comparison with other Downland landscapes, that of the Chilterns is ... unique."
(H. J. Massingham, in *Chiltern Country* [Batsford, London] 1940)

In south eastern Britain there are three principal ranges (or ridges) of chalk hills. (Perhaps four if the mid-range between north and south is counted. The most northern is the Chilterns. The others are, respectively, the North, Middle and South Downs.

The characteristic of this landscape is chalk hills, covered with a thin layer of soil, clay with flints, flint stone in abundance, and – in the Chilterns especially – deep gullies (or bottoms) more alluvial in quality, and steep-sided wooded valleys through which, in central and eastern areas, run vibrant, fast flowing streams, giving the Chilterns some of its unique quality. The characteristic does not occur in other chalk countryside, and is internationally rare.

Chiltern uniqueness: outstanding natural beauty

This landscape differs in other respects from that of Sussex, Hampshire, Wiltshire, East Anglia and other parts of southern and eastern England. For three quarters of their length – Totternhoe in Bedfordshire to the Thames at Streatley - the Chilterns' northern boundary is a steep escarpment overlooking the great Aylesbury Hundreds and the South Oxfordshire Plain. The feature has a parallel elsewhere in the long ridge of chalk that rises in Kent, peaking at Box Hill near Dorking in Surrey. On its south face, the scarp is more abundantly covered with grass and vegetation, attracting the farming of sheep.

Part of the Chiltern uniqueness is to be found also in the varied character of the great north-facing escarpment. Over a span of 35 miles the texture of the land changes: from the northeast, the Dunstable Downs and Ivinghoe's spare grass give place to the wooded environs of Coombe Hill, followed quickly by the dramatic sites of the Whiteleaf and Bledlow Crosses. Modern travellers using the road which parallels the scarp, and sometimes is called the Lower Icknield Way, are aware of the ridge: thick woodland alternating with open pastures as it sweeps on past Watlington Common towards Wain Hill. Thereafter the ridge falls away, as the land flattens and opens into a wide plain leading to the Goring Gap and the Thames; the river from here forms the southern boundary of the AONB and Society area.

Beyond the Goring Gap on the Thames the land rises steeply, rolling westward, first through beech woods opening out once more into grassed chalk downland. The Chiltern Ridge, the Upper and Lower Icknield Ways, used by men since Neolithic times, connects with the Ridgeway that continues westward to the Berkshire Hills, and into Wiltshire through Wayland's Smithy, Barbary Castle and Hackpen Hill. Here it merges with other great tracks converging on Avebury and Stonehenge.

How the Chiltern landscape was formed.

In a seminal work called simply *The Chilterns*, Leslie Hepple and Alison Doggett describe the great climatic and geological changes that ultimately produced the Chiltern landscape, and gave it its unique shape and quality. They record the discovery of early man's remains at Caddington clay pits, south of Luton, in layers of clay laid down during the Paeolithic Age, upwards of 100,000 years ago. These men were hunters who, as the climate became colder and worsened, died where they were, unable to migrate southwards to more temperate places.

"The most recent phases of geological history overlap with human pre-history. The periods with Ice Ages, the glacial, inter-glacial periods, and post-glacial, are central to the appearance and character of the Chilterns."

The alternate warming and cooling of the earth's surface, the destructive nature of frost and tundra, the movement of the crust, and the dust storms rent and stretched the surface of the Chiltern landscape. Warmth from the sun on southeast, south, and southwestern slopes softened ice and tundra. This caused a downward flow of soil and clay sludge that, over long spans of time, created the steep-sided valleys and 'bottoms' typical of Chiltern country. With the retreat of the ice, the climate and land grew warmer. The thaw released huge volumes of water that exploited weakness in the valley structure becoming the pro-genitors of fast flowing rivers and streams such as the Misbourne, Chess, Bulbourne and Ver. In the deeper, mostly western Chilterns, some valleys remained dry – the 'bottoms' of today. On the caps of many hills and valley ridges 'flint with clay' deposits and 'plateau drift' occurred, situations in which woodland could flourish, and especially the species which thrive there: the beech. Elsewhere, where the soil was deeper, oak, elm and birch were the colonisers.

Early settlement and the landscape's diverse character

A revolution in land use began in about 4000 BC with the arrival of Neolithic man. His predecessor Paeoliths and Mesoliths were primarily hunter-gatherers.The newcomers – their origin is uncertain - were farmers who created fields, cultivated crops and herded domesticated animals: sheep, goats and pigs.

"The whole degree and pattern of landscape impact changes with the beginning of farming in the Neolithic period (between 3500 and 4000 BC) when permanent settlement and cultivation first emerged."

Settlement, field demarcation, tillage, and herding were the characteristics of these new people.

Archaeological evidence of their presence in the Chilterns is relatively sparse, compared with, for example, the chalklands further south. Some authorities believe that they may have been more widespread but the sites and remains have been lost over the centuries, through urbanisation, ploughing and crop cultivation.

Bronze users, whose superior technology enabled greater woodland clearance, larger field cultivation, and significant advances in animal domestication, succeeded the Neolithic people. (The wheeled chariot first appears with these tribes who occupied many of the Neolithic sites between 1000 and 500 BC.)

Evidence of the settlements of Neolithic and Bronze Age communities in the Chilterns divides into three broad groupings. First, on the Thames gravels at Taplow, Hitcham area, Wallingford and North Stoke. Second, in the north Chilterns at Totternhoe, Dunstable and Ivinghoe. Third, in the Bledlow-Risborough gap – the broad lowland stretch which gives access to the Wye via the Saunderton-Bradenham valley. The Chiltern escarpment provided part of a communication route to and from the great cultural centres of Avebury, Stonehenge, and Silsbury Hill. Bronze users, and the Iron Age people who displaced them around 100 BC used the route also. This route (in the Chilterns, a broad span between what today is the Upper and Lower Icknield Way) began in East Anglia, and possibly further north, and followed the chalk hills through Norfolk, Suffolk and Cambridgeshire towards Hitchin. Here it continued onward into the Dunstable Downs, and thence westwards following the Chiltern scarp.

The Chilterns had great diversity because of the mixed and unexpected nature of the terrain. It was a region of open spaces where sheep could be run, of woodlands where pigs and hogs could be kept, of steep fields and spaces where cattle might graze, and of small villages and hamlets where, from Saxon times onward, people lived and worked in isolation. The region had abundant wild life; fox, badger and vole were typical and are still. Fallow and roe deer were common, to be joined in more recent Victorian times by the muntjac from China.

The 20th century - Massingham's Chilterns in the 1930s

In his introduction to his book *Chiltern Country*, H J Massingham describes the unique diversified nature of the Chilterns of the 1930s:

"Scattered over a breadth of from 15 to 18 miles there are huge areas of reddish, brick earth, almost as fertile as the Upper Greensand, whose boundary is more or less marked out by the entire course of the Upper Icknield Way from the Thames Valley to Dunstable. Reading Beds of a stiff marbled clay (also very productive when properly worked) occupy broad patches with out-liers in the south and east. Gault Studgy London clay, Thames alluvium, the sandy limestone or Totternhoe Stone, a clayey chalk (admirable for wheat and beans), tertiary deposits of gravels and clay-with-flints (bearing a luxuriant vegetation because of its richness in calcium) and pebbly glacial drifts which form a matrix for the silicate 'grey wethers' – all these pockets, patches, outcrops, smears, still further diversify the primal chalk.

"The consequences of this multiplicity of soils are, first, a higher ratio of fertility than in other downlands, and second, a greater variety of natural vegetation."

The Chilterns are not the 'exclusive kingdom' of the beech: only 'ash, larch and fir' are less common; the woodlands are mixed. Another effect, where not destroyed by urban development, is the richness and profusion of the flora:

"… orchises, mulleins, cranesbills, gentians, Daphne, clematis, wild columbine and certain rarities like coral root, golden saxifrage, *Daphnne mezereum*, the Great Pig Nut, the military orchis, winter green and others, nearly all gone. The Pasque Flower is not, I believe, found in the Chilterns proper, but years ago I saw it blooming on the Hitchen Downs. Hollies, wild gean, the cultivated cherry and the wild box still hold their own, but the juniper, older than the most ancient beech-forest is declining."

Chiltern traditional crafts and change

Massingham depicts the varied nature of craftsmanship that the prolific beech woods made possible: " … they supported a diverse company of bodgers, woodmen, and village craftsmen". These people used the wood to produce a variety of goods and resources needed by communities in the hamlets, villages and small market towns to be found throughout the Chiltern Hills. The woodlands were coppiced on an eight or nine year rotation for a variety of uses including charcoal making (a craft fostered and thriving today). Beech charcoal provided local fuel, the leaves for stuffing beds, the larger trees for bowls, the felloes for wagon wheels, barn-shovels and other implements, barn-floors and even house-beams; timber was chosen for the upper parts of chairs, the smallest for chair legs; the 'top and lop' for faggots." Massingham deplores the decline of such craftsmen as one outcome of the industrialisation of furniture making. Large-scale modern production relied increasingly upon imported timber. This affected and inadvertently conserved the Chiltern woodlands themselves.

Massingham also records, with regret, the changing circumstances and disappearance of other country crafts. Straw plait and lacemaking industries in Bedfordshire and especially around Luton where hat and bonnet making were staple; rush baskets and seats are gone. "Sandstone", he says, "is no longer quarried". Silk weaving at Tring, the Marlow wool fair, potteries at Medmenham, Coleshill and Chalfont St Peter, "the bell foundries of Little Missenden and elsewhere – all of these once thriving local industries", he says, "are hardly a memory". Other industrial-craft trades threatened or already vanished included the paper-mills of the

Chess, Misbourne and Wye; brickmaking and boot and shoe making at Chesham, though this town still boasts a thriving boot firm, well-known brickmakers and various wood-using firms.

The unique qualities of the Chilterns are also well exemplified in his description of their agriculture, as it was before the beginnings of modern farming methods took a deeper hold.

"Apart from woodmanship, agriculture, with its attendant crafts has been the staple industry of the Chilterns from prehistoric to living times. For this the variety of soils, the exceptional fertility of the bottoms and the base of the scarp and the turf-matting of the tilted sheepwalks are better adapted than are downs where more uniform geological conditions prevail."

A balanced husbandry was pursued by Chiltern farmers; "mixed farming with pigs foddered on beechmast, sheep folded or on sheepwalks, and Shorthorns on the hills". Market gardening was popular between the Thames and the escarpment; corn and fodder crops were rotated on the "well-watered edging of the Upper Greensand" and the Norfolk rotation of "wheat, oats, barley and leguminous seed crop, folded by sheep" was probably followed. Thus farming styles and methods, down the centuries, would have differed substantially from the processes common on the wider, more spacious uplands of England.

In many respects Massingham's description illustrates the ending of the long, slow, development of rural communities that reached a climax at the end of the 19th century. Production was primarily for local and home consumption, use and enjoyment: it sustained living at the customary level which, in the Chiltern country, as elsewhere in England, had gradually become more amenable, civilised and comfortable over the centuries. The pressures of rapid change, occurring in the great industrial towns of the North and Midlands were, in 1900, hardly felt in rural England. The pattern of life, despite a thousand years of transition, had changed relatively little since the Norman Conquest. Massingham writes of the "hour" of huge change to the countryside and its people.

The changes to the landscape, wrought since Massingham wrote, although great, have sustained still the claim for the unique nature and quality of the area. The creation of the Society in 1965, through the activities of Ted Castle and Christopher Hall established an instrument able to influence the direction of change to ensure the continuance and conservation of the Hills.

Doormouse from Bottom Wood

PART TWO

Transition – a new regime begins

During the three years that followed the foundation meeting, the Chiltern Society grew rapidly in numbers, approaching the first thousand by 1968. The variety of tasks it undertook was substantial; the old maxim that 'Nature abhors a vacuum' undoubtedly acquired a double significance. The initial building blocks, protest and anger, generated an enthusiasm that almost outran capacity.

The great achievements of these years were securing the early confirmation of the Chiltern AONB designation in late 1965, engagement with the M40 issues and the Pitstone Cement Works problem, and the rapid attack upon the deteriorating rights of way access. The Chiltern Society was making its presence known and seeking to establish its influence within the region. Christopher Hall described the process thus:

"Everything the Society did was publicised: a sharp campaign to ensure that planning applications were circulated to parish councils; an attack on Brakspear's Brewery for insensitive development of and around their village pubs ('Good beer, bad planning' was the Society's slogan); the cutting of wire on a public path at Wexham near Slough; support for the Milton Keynes plan to relieve pressure in south Bucks; a lost battle over a power line between Stokenchurch and Watlington; the successful shifting of a building ancillary to a gas pipeline from an unscreened to a screened site in the Turville valley; a highly successful intervention at the national level against footpath nationalisation which won us plaudits in a Parliamentary committee; the start of the Lacey Green windmill project ('sheer quixotry' Christopher Barry called it) under the aegis of the (newly established) Historic Works and Building Group (HW&BG); a row with the Nature Conservancy over access to Bald Hill on the scarp; the instantly successful launching of the footpath vigilantes scheme, a model of how publicity can generate voluntary effort; several major gravel extraction cases and many other issues."

An immense volume of activity for an organisation still in its infancy, and without – as yet, and not unsurprisingly so – certainty of direction and longer-term goals. This activity was supported by monthly meetings of the Executive Committee, a quarterly Council meeting representing the membership as a whole, and regular issues of *Chiltern News*, the magazine for all members, packed with information and trenchant views. The foundations were laid. However, there was also an uncertainty about the future; the pace was too fast; the risk of over-stretch was apparent. Christopher Hall acknowledges this in his conclusions:

"But it was all a strain. The first three years saw rapid expansion and the structure … could barely take it. The pressure of work on the Secretary and his wife and Jean Buchanan, the Field Officer, was immense. Relations with Bucks CPRE (which had refused to cooperate in appointing a member of the Joint Standing Conference of the AONB) were poor; the Chiltern Area Survey Commission (CASC), launched with enthusiasm, was running into difficulties as replies to its comprehensive questionnaire went for coding."

Seen in retrospect, the Survey demanded more of the young organisation than it could comfortably handle; it was running into difficulties as the returns of completed questionnaires flowed in. This compounded the unsteadiness and feeling of administrative overload, already apparent in other parts of the structure. It was, as Hall wrote, "time for a change"; time, perhaps, for some rationalisation and review of direction.

Christopher Barry, who had been one of the founding members, whose contribution in particular was the formation of the Historic Works and Buildings Group (HWBG), took over from Christopher Hall. He remained General Secretary until 1971, thereafter becoming Membership Secretary for a further four years. He consolidated much of the previous activity, smoothing and systematising the administration. He also sought to establish firm Groups to oversee Water Resources, Trees and Woodlands Conservation, Mineral Resources, and Anti-Litter. In this latter he undoubtedly had the energetic, committed support of Don Gresswell, who had joined soon after the foundation for whom this was a matter of great passion and concern.

The sufficiency and foresight of Barry's perception – if such justification were ever necessary, is the continuing concern that the Society has devoted to these important aspects of its activity. Readers of *Chiltern News* during the 1980s were familiar with the long struggle to save the River Misbourne, started and sustained by Vic Wotton for more than ten years, and later supported by Michael Rush. One result of this concern was that the Rivers and Wetlands Group now maintains a systematic watch on the Chiltern rivers, lakes and ponds to ensure both continuity of existence, as popular demands for water grow, and freedom from pollution. The Small Woodlands Scheme, now grown and extended into the Chiltern Woodlands Project Ltd, managed and directed by John Morris, is well known also. In 1965 the imminent expansion of Pitstone and Chinnor Cement Works provided the Society with one of its central activities at the time. The closure of the former almost 20 years later with the subsequent sale and development of the site has continued to be the Society's active concern. There were anxieties also about the volume of gravel extraction in the Thames valley to the southwest of the AONB; this also continues in the Society's watching portfolio. All owe much to the systematising and focus that Christopher Barry brought to the General Secretary's role and all this in addition to the major travail caused by the approaching M40, which loomed very close and large soon after he began his duties.

The role of the General Secretary

Peter Mould, Christopher's successor (1971-74) reflected upon the crucial role of the General

Secretary. In a way he saw it as one of part leader, part administrator, part sweeper, and part guardian. He wrote that a deliberate policy of delegation was essential, with a "massive effort to fill vacant posts" critical to the Society's continued health; he was also very sure that the job demanded of the post-holder was an:

"irreducible minimum of work which is more than most working people with family commitments could sustain for long."

He identified the principle functions as:
- Overall co-ordination of a variety of activities and the continuity of policy;
- The supplier of initiatives for new ventures;
- The recruitment of volunteers and helpers.

Often there was the additional need, through co-ordination, to ensure that focus was maintained in the Groups; this task changed as the Groups became more established and confident, and the General Secretary had to ensure that activity coincided with policy.

Prime responsibility for the execution of policy rested with the Executive (the Council was the policy making body) and it also had the duty of maintaining contact with civic and amenity organisations within the AONB. Thus, in carrying forward the task of administration, the Society's General Secretary became, in reality, its Chief Executive, reporting to its Board of Management. The function and role of the Secretary was one structural problem; the balance of responsibility between Council and Executive proved to be another.

Council, Executive or Executive Council?   Policy and balance.
This matter became prominent soon after Archie Campbell took over as General Secretary in 1974, serving until 1981. Archie, a retired senior civil servant, with experience of Government in Britain and in the colonies, met the criteria specified by his predecessor. He was retired, and notionally, had time to do what was undoubtedly becoming a substantial role. Archie Campbell described the position of the two controlling bodies as inherently defective. It was one the Society needed to address because of the press of business, and the frequent need for decisions of a policy-making nature. In turn, this skewed the intended balance between the Committee and the Council.

The latter comprised up to 30 elected members, officers from the Executive and specialist Groups 'ex-officio', and representatives nominated by each corporate member. The Committee was smaller, met frequently, and could act quickly. Archie's analysis pin-pointed the issues:

"… it was not possible to say whether the Council lacked grip and purpose because it met so seldom, (quarterly; the Executive met monthly) or whether the Committee assumed grip because it was

better informed. The fact remained that the Council withered whereas the Committee flourished."
(Vol.1 I, p.4)

A Forward Planning Committee had made a number of recommendations about the way forward for the Society at the end of its first ten years. It was aware of the changing balance between Council and Executive and:

"...... In an attempt to revive the patient, recommended travel and a change of air – the Council should meet at different locations and discuss a specific topic – a regimen that was intended to restore it to health. Unhappily it failed in its purpose. Attendance, averaging 28 between January 1975 and December 1976, fell to an average of 15 in 1977."

Archie Campbell had been optimistic at first about the change of strategy; *Chiltern News* in its 1976 AGM report records:

"The success in perambulating Council meetings was mentioned by the General Secretary ... It offered a better chance for local societies to meet the Society and to note matters in common."

A year later however it was proposed that the Council should be abolished. In February of the following year (1978), a special meeting was called at Watlington to review and determine the issue. On 25 February:

"It was then decided to let the old Council die, and to give to the Executive Committee the management of the business of the Society, renaming it the Executive Council. Members chosen by the four principal Groups of the Society would join the new Executive Council [previously these were not Executive members; a cause of some earlier dissatisfaction within the Groups] and, in order to provide a means whereby the affiliates could contribute to the Society's work, area meetings could be provided as necessary when the Executive Council sees fit."

The Executive Council, in essence, assumed the pattern of membership that it has retained and carried forward into incorporation as a Company limited by guarantee from July 1 2001.

These problems faced by the Society in the late 70s, are those that confront – and possibly still do – voluntary organisations whose officers and executive members are elected by a varied and disparate membership. The issues of effective governance, democratic control, policy determination and the capacity for – sometimes – rapid, yet fundamental decision-making touch the heart of voluntary commitment. The relationship of a 'governing council' to its membership, its executive and chief officer is one that has required attention during the past 30 years, by organisations large and small. The Chiltern Society was not alone in its endeavours to balance effectively the need for grass roots views to influence policy and decision-making.

The 10th Anniversary – a cause for celebration

During that first decade a solid base of environmental care and rescue work had been established. The 10th Anniversary was a moment to savour. It was specially marked by the Chilternscape competition, launched by the President, Lord Esher, and modelled on Art into Landscape, a successful Arts Council national competition held two years before. The design was to encourage schemes for improving local land and townscapes, and with support from companies and individuals who had close links with the Chilterns, to provide substantial cash and other prizes, for professionals, amateurs and school children. A sponsored walk organised for September 18 1976 and a party held at Bradenham Manor swelled the funds by £600 and a total of £1900 was set aside for prize money. Stephen Wright's professional scheme to enhance the waterside of the River Chess in Chesham, Bill Bruce's for the restoration of Turnpike Cottages at Henley, and the scheme by the pupils of Watlington School for the restoration of the local pond were the principal prize-winners. Lord Esher presented the prizes in the Spring of 1977; the entries were exhibited throughout the Chilterns.

Challenge and the future

In 1975 a Forward Planning Committee had reviewed the Society's direction, purposes, immediate and longer-term objectives. *Chiltern News* commented, "No Society such as ours can work without knowing clearly its aims." The Report, presented to the 1975 Annual General Meeting, set them out in some detail. These proposals were approved by the Executive Committee and formed a constructive platform for the incoming General Secretary.

- To work for an increased awareness of the Chiltern Hills as a distinct area.
- To increase the membership of the Society, particularly amongst young people.
- To increase the involvement and participation of members in the work of the Society, particularly on practical projects aimed at preserving or enhancing the landscape.
- To increase the financial resources of the Society to enable it to carry out its work effectively.
- To work for the observance and implementation of the Plan for the Chilterns and to secure a strengthening of the Chiltern Standing Conference and other consultative bodies.
- To secure strong and active representation of the Society on the Chiltern Standing Conference and other consultative bodies.
- To maintain and extend contacts with local government councillors and officials, and with MPs without losing the sense of creative independence.
- To identify and fulfil a distinctive role as a regional society serving affiliated local amenity societies and providing a link with various national amenity bodies. (9)

Commenting on these aims and objectives, in *The Chiltern Story 65-75* Peter Mould, who chaired the Committee, sounded practical and warm notes on the rallying trumpet:

"Precisely how to achieve all this will need to be worked out by the membership over the coming months and years. But, at this moment of time, on the 10th Anniversary, perhaps it is not immodest to suggest that the achievement which has followed from that beer between Chris Hall and Ted Castle, calls for celebratory drinks in the many excellent pubs throughout the Chilterns."

Writing in 2002, 27 years later, about the preparation for the Incorporation of the Society, Ray Challinor, the General Secretary, offered this observation:

"As we were undertaking a Strategic Review of the Society's present and proposed activities, the opportunity was taken to fine-tune the Objects as set out in the Constitution. Remarkably little was changed which is a tribute to the foresight of those founding the Society."

A strong position by 1981?

During the 16 years from inauguration, the Society's achievements included some heavy cases and fine causes. The spinal cord was the continuing, day by day, week by week, practical activity of the Groups: clearing footpaths, clearing litter, cleansing ponds, beginning to manage woodlands, contacting planning authorities, raising legal issues of access, gathering and submitting evidence, attending Inquiries, demonstrating and protesting where other means had failed – all in the interests of those who lived and worked in the area. The case of the M40 route through the escarpment was hard fought and in the end lost. There was successful resistance in 1972 to the proposed development of 350 acres of farmland for housing near High Wycombe, and modest, partial success in the case of unsympathetic housing development at Whiteleaf. The complete opening up of rights of way in the (then) 500 square miles of the Chiltern Hills was another fine achievement.

"At the final meeting of the *Countryside in 1970*, Don Gresswell, for the Rights of Way Group received the Duke of Edinburgh's Countryside Award, 1970, presented personally by Prince Phillip, for its survey, clearance and popularisation of Chiltern footpaths." (Vol.1, p.24)

The Society continued to seek improvements at the Pitstone Cement Works. It played a major role in the ultimate repair and adaptation of the Croxley Green tithe barn, preserving and renovating the exterior and converting the interior for use as a sports hall for the new Rickmansworth Grammar School. Above all it maintained a constant watch on the damaging progress of the M40 – seeking, where it could, to moderate its diminishment of the countryside. The fierce resistance to a service area at Stokenchurch is a classic example. Above all the Society sought to support and strengthen the Chiltern Standing Conference, a policy which, by 2001 saw achievement in the creation of the 'shadow' Chilterns Conservation Board, anticipating statutory status.

THE GREAT PROJECTS OF THE TIME (1968-81)

Five great projects were commenced during the first 16 years of the Society's life. Two were planned to celebrate the Queen's Silver Jubilee in 1977. Sarsen stones were placed in Wendover Woods to mark the occasion, and a formal survey of Chiltern Treasures and Eyesores was carried out with appropriate reports to parish and county councils that supported the project. The most ambitious and the earliest project, begun in 1971, was the restoration of the windmill at Lacey Green, finally concluded in 1986 – a great triumph.

The remaining two projects became independent incorporated partners of the Society, and are continuing to grow and develop as independent charities in their own right. Formal links are maintained with the Society through representation on their managing boards, and in many other ways. Those two are the Chiltern Open Air Museum Ltd at Chalfont St.Giles, from a move by the Society's HWBG, and finally opened to the public in 1981, and the Chiltern Woodlands Project Ltd based at Princes Risborough. It was constituted in 1989 from the Society's Small Woodlands Project originally started as a Government Community Programme. Both organisations, covering different subjects but both concerned with conserving the best of the built and the natural heritage, have achieved success as charities and companies limited by guarantee.

The Silver Jubilee of Elizabeth II – commemorative sarsens (1977)

For the Silver Jubilee of Elizabeth II, the Society engaged in a high profile collaborative venture to mark the occasion. Volume II of *The Chiltern Story* describes what happened.

"The Society played a leading part in bringing to completion the scheme of the Parish Councils of Halton and Aston Clinton to erect a cairn on the highest point of the Chilterns (not Coombe Hill) in the wooded hills above Wendover. This was a project carried out to mark Her Majesty's Silver Jubilee. With help from the Forestry Commission, the RAF, and the Jones Sand Company of Leighton Buzzard, four great stones were, after a five hour exercise of muscle and ingenuity, erected in the Forestry Commission plantation, and unveiled by the Lord Lieutenant of the County [Buckinghamshire], Major Young. If the weather had been clear enough and one's eyes were sufficiently perceptive, it would be possible to see across the North Sea and the North German plain, to Berlin, Warsaw and Minsk, from this cairn.")

The project, whilst not exactly a scheme of the moment was clearly one of inspiration and great daring. The event coincided also with the 10th birthday of the Society, itself the cause of some excitement and celebration. Archie Campbell ends his account with this note of admiration:

"A scheme such as this appealed to the imagination of Don Gresswell and the cairn marked (in an unobtrusive way, of course) a very high point in his organisational genius."

Treasures and Eyesores in the Chilterns – survey, record and action (begun 1977)

As its formal contribution to the Queen's Silver Jubilee year, the Society initiated this special project to survey and list man-made and natural Treasures throughout the area, and – in tandem – list those physical things and circumstances that could benefit the environment by their removal. It was intended that young people and adult community groups should be involved.

In 1977, Peter Mould, the originator of the project and the then Planning Adviser to the Society, wrote about the scheme:

"The project has yet to be formally decided but we envisage three stages. The first would be the survey itself which would result in completion of forms by parish councils, local amenity societies, schools, youth organisations and Society members who wish to volunteer for this work. We particularly hope to get young people involved in the survey work and will be inviting parish councils to play a co-ordinating role for their own parishes."

The next stage would cover the analysis of the reports. The results would be gathered in and sorted into categories, for example, historic buildings, historic monuments, attractive landscape features, hedgerows, ponds, roads, riversides, copses, country lanes etc. Treasures requiring protective action/listing, designation as a conservation area, Site of Special Scientific Interest (SSSI) status, tree preservation order or simply recognition of development control, would be so distinguished.

"The final, and by no means least important stage, would involve getting action. We would expect some of the organisations receiving reports to initiate action. The Chiltern Society's Conservation Volunteers Bureau would have a particularly important role, at this stage, in work on eyesores through its 100 or so registered organisations interested in practical voluntary conservation work. Most of these are youth organisations. The Chiltern Society Groups may also decide to engage directly in specific action and would be in a position to provide expert advice, particularly from its Historic Works and Buildings Group and Trees and Woodlands Group."

At the time the Society was not flush with money, so grants were applied for and received from South Oxfordshire and South Bedfordshire District Councils. Co-ordinators began work in three counties under the overall Project Co-ordinator, Vera Burden, and were given valuable help and support from parish councils, local amenity societies and schools. Begun in 1977, by late summer 1978, the Buckinghamshire survey was nearly complete; the Historic Works and Buildings Group was checking surveyed buildings for possible listing, and Don Gresswell's Conservation Volunteers had begun on the Eyesores. A generous grant of £1,000 from the Countryside Commission made possible the analysis and checking of the survey data. In 1979 the Society's then Chairman, Cllr Arnold Baines was able to present to the County the bound volumes covering the 57 parishes in Buckinghamshire. The Oxfordshire survey was presented to the Lord Lieutenant of the County in March 1980. At the end of 1980 Dacorum

Silver Jubilee fund gave £300 and this enabled work to be carried out in that area of Hertfordshire. The project as a whole was finally concluded in 1982, and noted by Charles Mills in Volume III of *The Chiltern Story*.

THE WINDMILL AT LACEY GREEN – A GREAT ACHIEVEMENT (1967-1986)

Less than two years after its foundation, the Chiltern Society became interested in the possible restoration of the mill. It is thought to be one of the oldest mills of its type in the country. It is a smock mill, with rotating top and fan-tail to turn it into the direction of the wind, and was a significant technical advance upon the older, traditional post-mill of which the Pitstone windmill is a fine example. The word 'smock' is commonly understood to refer to the traditional garment worn by farm workers that is similar to the shape of the tower. By 1915 the mill had ceased to work because it no longer had a viable economic use; the body rapidly decayed. A photograph taken in 1969 shows the tower with holes through the walls and the remnant of a sail. The fan-tail was missing but the cap, covered with corn sheets, remained as a valuable umbrella which probably saved the machinery inside.

"The windmill was in a state of rapid deterioration. The whole structure had become twisted and distorted and, although the original machinery was in a good state, weather was penetrating the cladding. Professional estimates placed the cost of restoration at £20,000 to £25,000 and there were considerable doubts as to whether the structure could be straightened."

The Society's Historic Works and Buildings Group decided to restore it so that it could be opened to the public. Local interest was stimulated and a lease signed in 1971.

"The plan, devised by engineer-in-charge Christopher Wallis, was to winch the mill upright so that the walls could be restored in situ by a team of volunteers. In addition to the voluntary labour, contributions in kind would be sought from firms to cut costs.")

A restoration committee was formed under the Society's Vice Chairman, Jeff Hawkins. A team of volunteers was gathered and the task of removing the cap and sails, and straightening the smock, was successfully completed in 1972. The Department of the Environment made a grant of half the estimated expenditure up to a maximum grant of £3,400, and no less than ten firms gave support in the form of equipment or materials, ranging from a crane to 100 year old wrought iron bolts.

"A wonderful concert in a barn at Hampden Bottom, given by Sir Bernard (later Lord) Miles and his wife on a summer's day in 1972 yielded nearly £500 towards the Society's share of the costs. Further collections were made in 1974 at open days for the public to view the restoration work and contributions were also received or promised from many individuals, from the Thames and Chiltern Tourist Board, and from Bucks County Council.

"The work was estimated to take four years with completion in 1976, although it may take a little longer than expected."

In 1981, Archie Campbell revealed a special personal interest in the project, devoting almost a full page in Volume II of *The Chiltern Story, The Next Six Years*, to the windmill restoration. Archie wrote:

"The Lacey Green Windmill is a story on its own and fully justifies the comment made by the Save Britain's Heritage (Campaign) in 1978 that it was a very splendid work that Chris Wallis and his team of workers were doing. It was hoped to finish the windmill – begun in 1971 – in 1977. 1981 saw the sails on, the weather-boarding painted and work still proceeding on the interior.

"Though much had been done, much remained to do, but by 1978 Chris was able to report that they had completed £70,000 worth of work for £3,500. The spirit that had inspired them cannot be better expressed than in the words of the master craftsman himself:

"It was all made by hand by men with simple tools, who grunted and struggled to make wrought timber, who sweated and measured and made mistakes cutting the joints, and finally succeeded in building their wooden monument nearly 300 years ago. It was this feeling that guided the philosophy of our restoration; it was the wish to retain the thumbprints of the men who made it which meant that it was essential to preserve the timbers themselves, rather than merely the form and shape of the structure. It was impossible to preserve rotten wood as such, but new pieces could be scarfed into members so that they could be fitted and joined in their original positions."

Archie's narrative continues:

"It is this feeling that has brought a bank manager, two teachers, a lecturer, a television technician, an ex-cocoa buyer, a bridge designer, not to mention the Deputy Director of Telecommunications at the Post Office, to devote their weekends, year in and year out, in rain and hail, snow and sunshine, cold and warmth, to the task.

"It should be noted that the restoration of the Lacey Green Windmill has been carried out to a specially high standard of workmanship and materials, and that the voluntary workers have taken infinite pains to do a good job. It is a notable achievement."

Another two years elapsed before the final peg was driven home and the formal official opening could be held. Soon after the AGM in 1981 Christopher Wallis wrote a column in *Chiltern News*, linked to a poem which epitomised the ten years of devoted, loving labour that the 20th century craftsmen of the Chiltern Society freely gave. This is what Christopher wrote and with it the words of volunteer David Empringham appeared in *Chiltern News*, Autumn 1981:

Lacey Green Windmill, by Christopher Wallis

When Elizabeth Stacey asked me to write something about the windmill to celebrate the new sails, my mind went completely blank. In the three years since the capping (putting on the roof) we made the sails, and then took months to complete the cap and tower so that the scaffold could be removed before the sails were hoisted.

I read my Lacey Green contribution for *Chiltern News* Issue No. 69 (Autumn 1978); what I said then applies now, except that the (nearly) total cost has doubled £7000. In the penultimate paragraph I looked forward to "eighteen months of real craft".

In 1978, although we had been working a craft, albeit a modern one, I enthused about the people who came together every Sunday to complete a seemingly hopeless never-ending task; not one mighty man, or two, but dozens, for one is nothing against such odds. These Chiltern Society men and women have continued to come and we have made many new friends, but I should like to devote this piece to the craft.

When restoring an ancient structure the best approach is "how much can be retained" not "how much can be renewed". These questions taken in reverse would quickly lead to a few old pieces of iron in a matrix of completely new timbers, and the character of the original maker's work, his thumbprint, would have been extinguished. To avoid this we have repaired the timbers of the structural skeleton individually before re-assembling them in their original positions; although this looks right, the resulting frame as a complete structure would have been very weak, and so we clad the whole with a stiffened plywood membrane concealed between two skins of weather-boards. The rest of the repairs, although visible are not intrusive and can only be seen after careful inspection. Woodworms seem to abound, but were baulked by the iron oak heartwood, and retired from the struggle many years ago, only leaving surface blemishes. Water is the greatest enemy of all timber structures, especially smock mills where it dribbles from top to bottom down the walls, running into any unseen cracks in the boards on the way. The Lacey Green boards were dried for years after sawing and all have been treated with preservative before assembly. The completed sails were dismantled and, together with the stocks, treated with preservative under pressure. A restoration by volunteers can afford to be perfect, for they will not do it for less.

All the external weathering details were designed to prevent completely the ingress of water into the timbers; the flashings down the corners, carefully fitted by John Harper and David Empringham, are not traditional, but are not obtrusive; they will last for ever, as will Graham Banfield's pressed aluminium roof, which looks like weather-boards.

There have been several staff changes recently; Bob Hussey has joined the veteran Mike Highfield to set up machinery for the working. Arthur Messer has joined Vic Day with the painstaking restoration of the internal wood "furniture". There is not space to name all those who have contributed their excellent work in the past, but I must mention the group from Flackwell Heath (Venture Scouts they were then) who pit-sawed all the sail timbers (aided and directed by me) and who played a large part in assembling the sails and moving them around the site for painting and so on.

This is the tenth year that we have "taken steel to wood". Soon, when this is finished, some of us will start again at Chinnor.

My mundane prose cannot pay fitting tribute to the grit and tenacity of our Chiltern Society workers who over the years have "carved their names on Lacey Green, with love". David Empringham's poem captures the spirit that has driven us, and will lead us onward.

Lacey Green Mill Reborn

Ten times the golden cups have filled
The meadows since the dying mill
First trembled to the touch of care,
Since to its drunk and sinking beams
The light of hope began to stream
And promise battened down despair.

Ten times the pines have tossed and quaked
While summer's finery was raked
Onto the ruthless levelling fire,
And from its pit of wormy oak
The phoenix in a fury broke
To wrest the wanderer from the mire.

Ten times the snows have veiled the smock
And filled the naked rack and lock
As men unbowed took steel to wood,
And as the wind from Aylesbury's plain
Shook the cap and frosted pane,
Gave their all for spirits' food.

Ten times the swallows here have flown,
Ten times the barley seeds been sown
While travellers on the distant vale
Have scanned the brow from "Pink" to "Whip"
On a word from half sure lips
To catch a longed for glimpse of sail.

Ten long years of sabbath days
Are numbered here of those whose ways
Will not perhaps be scribed above

But better still for they whose birth
Today will come, their name on earth
Is carved on Lacey Green with love.

And now the sails' new birth decree
With overwhelming symmetry
Let my heart with praises fill
For those whose work has here been done
And those who when grave battles swung
Gave shape and life to Lacey mill.

If Mother Shipton's words in time
Should all come true when in its chine
Poor Bledlow church will land
And earth will loose its shores,
There on a dark fantastic moor
A mighty mill may stand that needs a craftsman's
hand.

David Empringham

Work continued throughout 1982 and finally, on St George's Day 1983, Lord Bernard Miles formally declared the mill open.

"Many Society members were there on the great day and, of course, Christopher Wallis was among them. Lord Miles, in his speech, recounted a story previously unknown. In 1982, (he) and Lady Miles had given a second concert in aid of the Windmill fund; it was a grand evening. Afterwards Lord Miles gave the proceeds, £600, and as he walked away, said to his wife, 'It's a good idea, but they will never do it, you know.' Having told the story, he added how glad he was to have been proved wrong."

Reporting the occasion for *Chiltern News*, Pam Hawken added a dimension:

"In introducing Lord Miles to the 300 onlookers, Engineer-in-Charge Christopher Wallis said that they had sweated and struggled every Sunday in rain, snow, sun and wind for 12 years. This sunny afternoon was the celebration of their achievement. After Lord Miles had finished speaking, the great white sails were released and triumphantly turned against the blue sky. The old mill, idle since 1915, was alive again in the wind. The day concluded with an entertainment given for the workers and their families by Lord Miles and his wife (actress Josephine Wilson), and an English village tea prepared by the ladies of Lacey Green and Loosley Row."

At the Annual General Meeting in 1986 it was announced finally that the work was fully complete; the scaffolding had been removed, the cap was free to turn in any required direction and the machinery was in full working order. In the same year a Malcolm Dean Design

Award was given to the Society for the windmill's restoration. The presentation was made at Lacey Green on March 19 1987, by the Chairman of Wycombe District Council. Christopher Wallis received the Award on behalf of the Society but also was awarded a personal Certificate in recognition of the immense contribution he had made to the success of the project.

CONCLUSION – 1965-1981 – MANY ACHIEVEMENTS AND MUCH SATISFACTION; A WARNING NOTE

During its first 16 years of life, the Chiltern Society, working with local amenity and environmental organisations, became a significant regional conservation organisation. It tackled, with considerable success, a variety of planning issues concerned with development, such as house construction, the siting of buildings, insensitive placement of utility supports, land use problems, proposed road development and many others. Towards the end of that period the issue of aircraft noise and airport development began to loom ever larger.

The Society had early undertaken a massive rights of way clean up to restore the Chiltern network, and to create a supervising system that would ensure continuance of access. In retrospect the great battle over the M40 and its devastation of the escarpment may, nonetheless, have helped to ensure the greater harmonic quality of the eventual A41 trunk road development during the 90s. In addition to creating an effective planning watch with an adviser and a Chilterns-wide team of volunteer Field Planning officers, success was gained fighting several large attempts to urbanise distinctive rural and farmland locations, especially in the surroundings of High Wycombe. Two remarkable achievements came from this period: the creation of the Chiltern Open Air Museum for historic buildings, and the partial restoration of the smock mill at Lacey Green, finally completed in 1986. The former was within the space of three years, the latter spanning almost 20. These are immense tributes to voluntary effort and persistence of spirit.

In concluding his volume about his six years of tenure, Archie Campbell recorded his belief that the climate and attitude of Government and society towards the environment had changed. The Society, he says, faced a more favourable situation in 1981 than existed at its founding in 1965. He instances the recent Countryside Commission Report, and the fact that two more AONBs have been established … " as evidence of a better, more friendly climate. The change of emphasis in the Countryside Commission's work from recreation to conservation is most heartening".

However, he also believed that pressures were building: for more houses, and for the resuscitation of rural communities through industrial development. There were schemes to enable faster motoring, and to create greater space for countryside recreation – "which will all necessitate vigilance". He ends by saying that the voluntary movement will be looked to, to take more of the burden and be expected so to do. His forecast proved right as legislation for education, the social services and the environment after 1981 underlined.

In a final word he touches what was, during his last year, an issue which had been noted at Annual General Meetings by Bill Bruce, the Treasurer in 1978 and 1979, the need to increase membership. From around 2,700 in 1974, it had risen to just under 3,500 by 1981. The Treasurer had reminded the AGM in 1977, when a small operating surplus was reported, that membership income was crucial to the continuance of the Society in the range of work it carried out. Archie wrote:

"This makes enlisting support for recruitment the most urgent task . Our numbers have remained just a little better than static for the last six years – it has taken a great effort by a few people to make progress. We still remain among the first five or six amenity societies in the UK in terms of numbers, and probably not inferior to any in terms of reputation and effectiveness. But neither status can be maintained without more support from the hundreds of thousands of people who live in the Chilterns. It is up to our members to enlist them."

Charles Mills, who joined the Executive Council in 1978, began to systematise recruitment. The task continuing to be a major priority for him on becoming Chairman in October 1981.

Grange Farm, Maidenhead by Lorna Cassidy

PART THREE

GROWTH AND RESPONSIBILITY (1982-1993)

PERSPECTIVE IN 1982

In 1982, Archie Campbell began writing the history of his time. (Volume II *The Next Six Years*) He was elected to office in 1975, just as Britain was entering a time of economic, social and cultural change; two previous years of oil crises had heightened the national mood of an uncertain future. For the Chiltern Society some consolidation, stability and administrative balance were essential.

Archie had been a member for several years, and by training and experience had soon grasped the issues facing the Society. His subsequent achievements to introduce and maintain a steady state carefully prepared the way for further advance when the moment came.

Four years into his term a change of Government brought a more radical national agenda for voluntary organisations. The Government's policy was to encourage a greater voluntary response to community needs. Archie saw in this as an enlivening opportunity for the voluntary sector and expressed his view that voluntary service and volunteering had a positive future. However, towards the end of his tenure, he also suggested that this could lead to the overload of volunteer workers. This was particularly true of environmental groups like the Chiltern Society. (Vol II pp.20-22)

The six years of his Secretaryship were busy ones; there were uncertain times, when Archie of necessity also became Editor of *Chiltern News*. But there were far more successful ventures: Don Gresswell's Silver Jubilee project excited him, and he found quite remarkable the speed with which Dick Amsden and his Historic Works and Buildings Group colleagues launched the Chiltern Open Air Museum. He wrote, "it had found an early coming of age and had rapidly outgrown its parent". (Vol II.p10)

Nevertheless uncertainties existed, that required a steady hand. In the Executive Council there were differences of opinion and doubts about the best way for the Society to grow; what should be done about involving the membership who, because they were represented on the Council, were the policy makers. Archie's Editorial duties made substantial demands and it was not until the appointment of Elizabeth Stacey as Editor, at the end of his office term in 1981, that relief came.

Membership rose but slowly: by 1975 it stood at 2,700, and by 1981 it was 3,415, a five year net gain of only 715, which Archie considered unsatisfactory but not to be dismissed as the result of neglect.

There were other unsure situations for voluntary associations. After 1974 the impact of Local Government Reform in the shire counties was apparent in many organisations associated with the countryside and environment. The new authorities were in their infancy throughout Archie Campbell's term of office. The Chilterns had four County Councils and 11 District Councils with which new connections had to be made to replace former and possibly, long-standing ones.

Towards the end of the six years of Archie's service these problems were compounded by the changing industrial and economic circumstances of the country. Inflation, the rising cost of living, and the pressures that these matters exerted within families tended to make people reluctant to commit themselves and their time to voluntary work, unless it directly benefited the family.

Membership – a matter of prime concern

Membership was the major problem facing the Society during the late Seventies and into the next decade. Bill Bruce, the Treasurer regularly reminded the Executive Council that membership subscriptions were the Society's largest source of income; it was more than 60% dependent for survival on a steadily increasing membership.

Charles Mills joined the Executive Council in 1978, and immediately offered to tackle the problem of falling membership. This objective he pursued steadily throughout his 18 years on the Executive Council, almost to the time of his death in 1997. His persistence was rewarded: by 1986 membership exceeded 5,000. Recruitment eased off during the subsequent two years and Charles, by then a Vice President, reminded the EC in 1988 that continued progress was important and required constant attention. He welcomed the Chairman's (Harry Cook) initiative to propose the appointment of Edward Newmark as Membership Secretary from June 1990.

Charles' first strategy had one unifying theme: involve the members, work through them. He planned a series of presentations to groups and organisations likely to be interested and where cross membership was probable. These were successful; however when the arithmetic was done it was found that gains were still more or less neutralized by losses. An alternative way was needed.

Membership: campaign and involvement; successful recruiting

The next campaign involved members more closely. Charles Mills described the process and outcomes:

"The new system soon ... gave indications of success. Two or three meetings were held each year. Names of people were obtained from *Chiltern News* deliverers, relating to the area in which the team was working. Letters were sent to those members who were asked to reply; in the absence of a reply a follow-up telephone call was made. A better-known member was asked if the meeting could be held in his house. His name appeared as the signature on the invitation letter.

"The team (led by Pam Hawken) always attended the meeting. ... From then membership improved steadily, and in1986 the total exceeded 5,000." (Vol III p.30-31).

Pam had been a successful recruiter in the Chorleywood area and brought her experience to the larger scale task, continuing an ardent activist and promoter of the cause for the next ten years. She coupled with it other promotional events: the identification of suitable Conference locations, support for the Society`s sales section, and responding to issues in the local or national press.

There were two developments of this strategy that added strength to the efforts and some impetus. In 1981, under the new Editor, Elizabeth Stacey, *Chiltern News* was given a livelier format and popular style. Throughout all subsequent editions the membership campaign received a higher profile. The other strategy was to change the AGM format, to make it more attractive to members and enable their greater participation. The Annual Report for 1982/83 carries Charles Mills' explanation of his purpose:

"The AGM this year begins at 11.00am with a lunch break at 12.30 – 2 p.m. The intention is to give members more time to present their points of view, to raise matters under any other business, and to make it a more attractive, social occasion." (CN No. 90.)

The *News* headlined the AGM Notice with Let the Members Talk, and the rank and file received it well. However, the change did not work quite in the manner intended. The next Annual Report (1983/84) includes a note by Charles at the end of his Introduction, a little tongue in cheek possibly although of stern intent:

"The AGM this year, as last, starts at 11am. Lunch will be obtainable at the venue. Last year`s proceedings were curtailed because several speakers, mostly Group officers, spoke for too long. Verbal reports by officers are intended to be confined to matters not included in the published reports, and should be brief and to the point. This year I shall apply time limits strictly and trust that you will bear with me." (Annual Report 1983/84 in *Chiltern News* No. 94. p12)

This was his last year as Chairman, but the Meeting expressed continued confidence in him by electing him Vice Chairman for 1984/85. Charles Mills remained on the Executive Council, representative of the Trees and Woodlands Group, and a Vice President of the Society until his death in November 1997.

NEW PROJECTS TO STIMULATE AND ENCOURAGE GROWTH

Charles Mills had reflected on the Society's need for new projects. He wrote:

"Much routine work was going on within the Groups in 1982 but there was a feeling that new projects were needed to restore the old fire and enthusiasm that had started the Society, which this time seemed to be in decline." (Vol III. p2)

Steps and Stiles

Don Gresswell's Rights of Way Group Steps and Stiles Project generated some new activity, although work had barely begun in 1982. Don had designed a simple, pre-fabricated stile incorporating a vertical handrail. He proposed a review of all Chiltern stiles, and afterwards, to fit a step to each that lacked one. Where a stile was found defective it was intended to replace it with another of the new design. The work was to be taken on by the footpath officers from the ROWG supported by the Conservation Volunteers. Don paid for and provided the steps, and Bucks County Council provided the rest of the woodwork. This practical project re-ignited some of the old fire and enthusiasm, bringing satisfaction to Group members.

Small Woodlands Project

To generate activity and interest even more Charles Mills introduced a new scheme: the Small Woodlands Project. Its purpose was to assist and encourage Chiltern owners to manage and maintain their woodlands in a satisfactory and ecologically sound way.

The need at the time was urgent. There were, and remain today, possibly because of the energy with which the Project was pursued, 16,000 hectares of woodland in the Chilterns. 8,500 are classified as 'ancient woodland', that is, 300 or more years of age. The ultimate success of this project, now a company limited by guarantee and a registered charity, is described in Part Four of this History, and in *History in Chiltern Woods* by John Morris, who was appointed Project Manager, and remains so to this day.

The Project was set up under the aegis of the Manpower Services Commission Community Programme, established by Government in 1973, as a means of easing the levels of unemployment by training or retraining those people whose jobs had been lost.

The Small Woodlands Project succeeded and survived, overcoming crisis when the MSC began to wind down, by developing consultancy work, and a management advice service to owners. Other support came from the Countryside Agency, the Forestry Commission, Bucks County Council and District Councils in Buckinghamshire, Hertfordshire and Oxfordshire.

In describing the negotiations that later helped to establish the Project on a stronger financial footing, Charles Mills recorded an instance of the shrewd business sense and generosity of Don Gresswell who had taken a keen interest in the Scheme.

"In June 1983 the Chiltern Standing Committee met the Society, approved the Project and asked for financial help from Chiltern Local Authorities. This was agreed. As we were waiting for the reaction to the request for money, Don Gresswell said quietly to Charles Mills, sitting alongside, "Tell them the Society is putting up £500, that should persuade them", and so it did. He provided the £500 from his own money." (Vol III, p.23)

A generous gift: Bottom Wood

During 1981/82 Derek Martin, Vice Chairman of the Society had met Cynthia and Lucien Ercolani (the maker of ERCOL furniture), who owned Bottom Wood, Radnage, near Stokenchurch. Cynthia had maintained the Wood as a small sanctuary for wild life, but for several years it had not been effectively managed. Derek had discussed with the couple the possibility of transferring the Wood to the Society to enable it to be cared for by the Trees and Woodlands Group.

Early in 1983, Charles Mills' plans for the Small Woodlands Project were well advanced, and he now needed a wood in which to organise the training of the supervisor and six trainees approved by the Manpower Services Commission's Community Programme. Derek suggested the possibility of Bottom Wood for this purpose, and introduced Charles to the Ercolanis. They favoured the idea, intimating also that they were proposing to present the Wood to the Society. On 22 August 1983 the Project Team, under their newly appointed manager, John Morris, began operations in Bottom Wood. By the first months of 1984 the gift of the Wood to the Society was complete and its continued management by the eventually reconstituted Chiltern Woodlands Project Ltd commenced.

From the time of its gift it gave a much-needed boost to the interests and activities of the Society, as well as a valuable training ground for the newly established Small Woodlands Project. Writing in 1993, Charles Mills proudly summarised the Project's results:

"In the ten years since the Society assumed ownership the work of removing dead trees, thinning unwanted trees, and felling several groups of over-mature trees has gone ahead. Bottom Wood is now in prime condition and recently it has been said that no further major work needs to be done for several years."(Vol III.p22)

Money was spent on improving paths through the Wood, and an information board for visitors was erected. The costs of the entire operation, over the decade, were met from selling timber – "well over £1000." – with enough over to assist funding of future work.

Membership – a matter for persistence and patience

Membership, its consolidation and steady increase, continued to be a major concern for the Society. It had been part of the commitment made, and the three-fold strategy employed by Charles Mills from the time he joined the Executive Council and throughout his long involvement with their work. He had streamlined the administration and with the diligent research support of the Treasurer, Roger Hill, the first Society computer was purchased in 1984 allowing for more efficient record keeping.

He became concerned again in 1986, when a strategic change in recruiting policy seemed to have occurred. He wrote:

"… the recruiting team (having reached the 5000 goal, felt that after eight years constantly repeating the same message, it was time for a new team with fresh ideas to take over. Sadly there was no move to restart the programme for the next two years." (Vol III.p31)

He was not wholly right; an effort was made. *Chiltern News* (Winter 1986) promoted the launch of Pam Hawken`s campaign for the placement and monitoring of recruitment leaflets in libraries and their branches throughout the AONB. This was only partly successful, being reliant upon the good will of library staffs, who had to find time to top up display stands.

A more systematic programme began in 1991 under the aegis of chairman Harry Cook. Following the success of small local experiments by Don Millar posting membership leaflets into neighbouring houses, he obtained a donation from British Airways to fund the cost of more circulars, as well as his general conservation work. With a new Membership Secretary in charge, Edward Newmark, who was much impressed by this success, the programme was extended on a much wider scale during the following 21 months, using the Royal Mail Door-to-Door service. 213,296 newly designed leaflets were despatched; the response was dramatically high, approximately seven per thousand and produced over 1400 new members, including 40 new Life Members. When the pace eased, Charles Mills commented yet again to the Executive Council that constant attention was needed if a steadily increasing membership was to be achieved.

However, due both to the energy of Captain Cook, the Chairman, and Edward Newmark's tenacity, the drive for membership was never far from anyone's minds. Harry Cook's successor, Barry Scott sustained the campaign, as numbers still only totalled some 5000, and continued under Michael Rush who also introduced a constructive approach to marketing the Society more widely and systematically.

Charles Mills' influence upon the Society extended well beyond the areas for which he took special responsibility; his influence and activity undoubtedly gave the Society the base and focus it needed to move forward into the last years of the 20th century and the new Millennium.

The combination of his perception, and that of Harry Cook, who stirred the Society from a relative torpor, together with the steadying hand of Barry Scott, created the foundation on which Michael Rush could build on his election to the Chair in 1997.

AN UNCERTAIN HORIZON: PERSPECTIVE IN THE LATE EIGHTIES

Charles Mills' immediate successor was Wing Commander Derek Martin (1984/87).He brought to the task more than ten years' experience of the Society's business. Derek had been first secretary of the fledgling COAM (1975/76), and Planning Adviser in succession to Peter Mould in 1982. His personal links with Lucien and Cynthia Ercolani facilitated the successful transfer of Bottom Wood to the Society in 1983. He had played a considerable part in sustaining the Society's influence in the Chiltern Standing Conference, and with its constituent local authorities. He was also a successful membership recruiter in campaigns between 1980 and 1983. Derek Martin's election was fortunate at this time of uncertainty about the future safety and conservation of the Chilterns landscape and natural environment. He was well briefed by his knowledge and sharply aware of the difficult issues facing the Society's future.

His three Annual Reports contain much reference to the need for conservation and resistance to perceived threats to the AONB from many sources. His speech to the 1987 AGM summarised his concerns:

"As I said in my report we face increasing pressures. Extension of the M40 to Birmingham will increase pressure for offices, industry and housing. Already we are opposing the motorway service station area near the Chiltern escarpment.

"In the south of our area there is still the threat of the bridge across the Thames east of Reading, the gradual expansion of Reading into the Chilterns area, and the possibility of a link road between the M4 and the M40. In the north we have the possible expansion of Luton airport.

"Over the whole area we have increasing pressure from housebuilders, from High Tech Business and Industry Parks, from Campus Office developments ... the list is endless. One of the greatest sources of pressure is the food mountain and the consequent (need for) reformation of the Common Agricultural Policy."

The speech reflected many of the political pre-occupations of the times; how could this small island accommodate the expanding demands of the high tech industries? What should be the housing policy for the over populated South East? Would Government proposals not create a linear town from somewhere near Slough to the outskirts of Swindon? Would small industrial (craft and art or simple engineering work) workshops, using redundant farm buildings, help to re-generate the rural economy and communities? How ought we to meet the growing need for new homes and ease the pressures upon our inadequate road system?

This was the time when the decision was taken to complete the M25 as the answer to London traffic congestion. It was the beginning of debates leading to the final decision on the A41 north from Watford. Elsewhere in the South East, the Newbury by-pass issue was being fought out. Beyond this was the widening and dualing of the London to Exeter road. Derek Martin was reflecting and expressing some of the anxieties that worried the Chiltern Society membership at the time. These concerns were reinforced by Harry Cook as he became involved in the Society's business after his election in October 1988. However the Society also took time out to celebrate its growth and achievements.

21ST (1986) AND 25TH (1990) ANNIVERSARY CELEBRATIONS – PARTY TIME

The 21st Birthday was celebrated in "grand style". Pam Hawken reporting for *Chiltern News* began her description in lyrical mode.

"It seemed as if even the sun was helping the Society to celebrate on July 19. On a lovely summer evening members strolled about the idyllic grounds of Pipers Corner School, Great Kingshill, with its extensive views over the Chilterns, to the music of the Owlswick Quintet. They enjoyed drinks from the bar and a delicious supper prepared by the ladies of the Society, and afterwards listened to madrigals given by the Henley Singers.

"And the Society was celebrating with justification: since 1965 the handful of founder members has grown to over 5,000. And it has a wonderful record of achievement, all done by volunteers who feel strongly about saving the Chiltern countryside for future generations. On many occasions it has been only the Society that stood to safeguard some part of the Green Belt, some historic building, some wood or footpath.

"The Society Groups were represented by their Display Stands; there was a tombola, a slide show of the Society's work, and Christopher Barry, a long-serving Officer of the Society, acted as MC.

"Wing Commander Martin thanked everyone who had helped to make the party a success, and after Chris Hall (first General Secretary) had cut the birthday cake, he gave the Toast **"The Chiltern Society"** in which all present warmly joined." (CN.No.102)

The event four years later at Fingest followed a very different, but equally enjoyable course. The report was written by Elizabeth Owen, who began also with an appreciation of the fine weather on that early autumn day.

"In lovely weather the occasion began with a walk led by Ken Poyton through the local countryside. He brought us safely back to a welcome cup of tea prepared by a galaxy of organisers led by Cic Upcott, Joan Morris and Di Millar. More and more members were arriving by the minute, ... We then enjoyed ourselves by roaming abound the ancient (Manor Farm) barn, chatting with friends and making new acquaintances ... admiring the watercolours by Joanne Nicholl, on display. The picture quiz was won by Helen Willson, a long-standing member of the Society.

"... prompt on time ... with corks popping and surrounded by beautiful flower decorations   created by Elsie Poyton, the party sat down to enjoy a mouth watering barbeque prepared by Derek Upcott assisted by Pip Barston, an on-the-spot volunteer. I heard many people vowing that they never ate trifle but the sight of 22 assorted and beautifully presented bowls obviously inspired even the faintest heart (for we couldn`t possibly have been hungry still) and every scrap went. 120 people were feasted."

Entertainment was provided by the Chesham Light Opera Company with excerpts from musicals and a monologue in the style of Alan Bennett. A short speech by Charles Mills, a visit from Derek Martin, the cutting of an enormous birthday cake and champagne rounded the evening off. A raffle brought a "handsome donation" to the Society's funds.

> "So the evening closed, the raffle prizes drawn, the farewells said, and in a state of mild euphoria we made our way under a starry sky to our cars waiting in a neighbouring field." (CN No.118).

A new Chairman - changing pace and raising the public profile

Captain Harry Home Cook RN (ret'd) had been a member of the Water Resources Group, having an interest in the revival of Chalfont Park Lake. He brought to his new task as Chairman the brisk approach traditionally associated with experienced naval officers, and the tenacity of a serviceman accustomed to achieving goals and targets. His good humour and his humanity were apparent, as were the decisive qualities of a person at ease with himself; confident of the direction in which to go. He applied these attributes directly to the Chairman's role he had accepted.

During his term he frequently held meetings at his home entertaining members of the Executive Council and Groups, where his wife 'Fania always provided refreshments. Her strong, dedicated interest in the Society was illustrated by Christopher Tatham, retiring General Secretary, at the 1993 Annual General Meeting. She had hosted 75 meetings during the year and in a tribute to her, Christopher said, "She has done an enormous amount to raise the morale of the Society."

The *Chiltern News* cover for September 1990 illustrated an occasion of Harry and 'Fania Cook`s hospitality, showing a tea interval during a Planners' meeting held at their Layters Green home. Harry Cook retired from the Chair in1993 having served one year more than he originally intended, and brought about a number of changes upon which the Society could build.

Support and Information Local Members' Groups

Harry Cook believed that the Chiltern Society needed deeper roots amongst the membership and in local communities that make up the Chiltern Society and its area. He decided this was achievable by setting up groups in districts that seemed likely centres of action. Models existed in a strong, established group at Marlow, led then by a dedicated Society member, Ken Poyton, and in Berkhamsted, led by Roger Hill.

When explaining his purpose to a local press reporter, he said he felt communication between members was a problem. By setting up Support and Information Groups he was:

> "…trying to introduce his members to one another so that the organisation of environmental projects, such as pond clearance, can run smoothly without him having to make 100 phone calls to get a handful of strangers together."

With this objective in mind he revived earlier attempts to establish local groups, giving them an enhanced role under the title of Support and Information Groups (SIGs). During the next three years 16 of these were organised, each with their own officers and regularly supplied with Chiltern Society updated membership lists.

Analysis and lifting the public profile and image

With the help of Roger Hill, the Treasurer, Harry made an early examination of the Society`s financial position, and its recruitment procedures. He argued and won the case for an increase in the annual subscription, which was doubled from 1 July 1989.

It was decided to make another drive to increase membership, and a small working group led by Ken Poyton and Cic Upcott produced a plan for a widespread poster and leaflet distribution, a speakers' list to enable response to organisations expressing interest, and coffee mornings to be provided by the developing S & I networks. The plan also included the first of a number of hands-on appearances at a local supermarket, what the Chiltern News later headlined as:

"A Chiltern Society Display at ASDA. The Society shop was the 29th Till!"

The report continued:

"The event raised the profile of the Society in High Wycombe and produced a number of new subscribers. In addition 268 footpath maps, 61 desk jotters, and 132 tea towels were sold together with a clean sweep of 350 lovely greetings cards." (CN.No114)

The success encouraged a similar venture at Worlds' End Nurseries, Wendover. 30 members responded to the request for speakers, and 200 organised a poster distribution in their home area. The Executive Council considered the work well founded.

The Ken Poyton/Cic Upcott working group report also said that the Society would need to recruit about 700 members to sustain its development, and that it hoped there would be more younger people coming forward "as we are an ageing society". The committee members were aware of contemporary British and Western European demographic trends and the ageing population in many advanced societies world wide.

Harry Cook believed that the public profile of the Society ought to be more prominent. To this end he proposed a patron of distinction should be sought. He consulted Lord Esher, the retiring President who was standing down in October 1990, having served in that capacity for 25 years. Lord Esher approached Her Royal Highness, the Duchess of Kent who accepted the role for an initial period of five years, later extended for a similar term. The election of Sir Leonard Figg, a prominent Buckinghamshire landowner as President, added a further dimension to the higher public status that Harry Cook considered essential.

Planning for the Chilterns of the future

Since it began, the Society had worked within the Standing Conference for the Chilterns (previously known as the Standing Committee). Soon after the Society was founded it sought links with the Conference, and aimed to enhance its work and standing; it shared this purpose with other local environmental bodies. The AONB required a strong Conference that would have authority and clout, and a care brief touching issues of planning, development, leisure and recreation, and the environmental quality of the Chiltern countryside.

At the time, the Conference was not a strong organisation and was without statutory authority, although there were representatives from four County Councils, the Forestry Commission, the Countryside Commission and the Nature Conservancy. It had no powers to secure or enforce its proposals.

A first *Plan for the Chilterns* had been produced in 1971, with much support from the Society, and there was hope that this would give guidance to "local planning authorities in their decisions".(Vol 1.p21)

Peter Mould, the then Society's General Secretary, welcomed the fact that there was a plan and an objective. Nevertheless he noted a number of critical points:

"...wishy-washy" proposals for agricultural and farm buildings;

...the absence of any firm proposals for the creation of a sense of identity (eg. warden service, roadside signs);

...the absence of any proposals for ensuring effectiveness in implementation (eg. by AONB planning staff responsible to the Conference, or a joint planning committee)."

Peter concluded that:

"The Society has been fortunate in having representatives on the Conference's Participation Panel who have made these points both in committee and in public." (Vol.1 p21)

The interest generated by the 1971 Plan was not followed by significant action. Local Government Reorganisation in 1974 had had the effect of breaking long established contacts and working patterns, and Government attitudes towards the voluntary sector were once more changing, as has been noted already. In 1982 Archie Campbell comments a little wearily on the demands being made.

"We already carry out Highways work in our footpath clearance, Department of the Environment work in our vigilance over ancient buildings, and County Council work in keeping the Chiltern Standing Conference alive; we shall be called upon to do more." (Vol II, p22)

And so it began to be proved; the ideas of the mid- and late Victorians about self help and social responsibility regained ground. However, not deterred by this shift in Government attitude, the Society held to its objective of working for a strong statutory Standing Conference.

Almost as part of this purpose and soon after Harry Cook's tenure began it was decided to increase the number of volunteer Advisers to the Executive Council. This strengthened the Society`s capacity to collaborate with the Conference. The existing Advisers specialising in Planning and the Green Belt were already heavily committed; the problem of aircraft noise, airport expansion and the issue of the fifth terminal for Heathrow were each making heavy demands upon time and energy.

Three new appointments were made: John Knight (Farming), Peter Mansell-Moullin (Minerals), and Dr Barry Scott (Roads) who was also a member of the Standing Conference`s Technical Panel.

The New Management Plan for the Chilterns (1994)

In 1992 the Chiltern Standing Conference met at Green Park, Aston Clinton; the subject was *The Chilterns: What Future?*

The objective was to consider the shape and scope of a future management plan for the Chiltern Hills, to review the old Plan of 1971 and to determine areas of improvement. The principal contributors were Harry Cook, Richard Mabey, author and environmentalist, Kevin Haynes, and Michael Gwilliam, Bedfordshire's Chief Planning Officer who chaired the Conference. (Eight years later Michael Gwilliam was to become one of the principal executives in the new South-East Region of Government.) He claimed that:

"…this new Plan for the Chilterns will be up to date, will have more vision and will be better than that for a National Park." (For several years there had been a modest lobby for National Park status for the Chiltern AONB.)

Some weeks later, at the Society's Annual meeting in 1992, Harry Cook was able to tell members of the very positive advantages of continued involvement in the development of this new Plan. The Conference's Technical Panel, on which the Society representatives sat, now had four new working groups to prepare the Plan`s framework. Chiltern Society members appointed to these groups were Christopher Morris to Development; John Stidworthy (Chairman of theTWG) to the Woodlands group, itself led by Sir Leonard Figg (Society President); John Knight (Farming Adviser) to join the Farming working group; Dr. Leslie Drain (from the ROWG) to join the Downland study group.

Harry Cook concluded his observations with a characteristically challenging statement:

"This is indeed a major step forward, and we must make absolutely certain that we keep this relationship because at the end of the day we still have to work through the Standing Conference if we are to achieve our aim, which is to strengthen the Area of Outstanding Natural Beauty and our own area which includes the Green Belt and its fringe." (AGM Minute, 1992)

In October 1993 the draft *New Plan for the Chilterns* had been widely circulated.

Christopher Morris prepared a summary and leaflet for distribution; members were urged to respond quickly to the consultation. The Society also received a letter from Michael Gwilliam expressing great appreciation of the cooperative support given to him by its members, during the Plan's preparation. He looked forward to an even closer working relationship.

He wrote again to the President, Sir Leonard Figg, regretting that he was not free to attend the AGM, but renewing his warm thanks for the Society's help throughout the year. He made a special acknowledgement of Christopher Morris and Barry Scott's work, for members're-sponses to the consultation and finally for the financial contribution made by the Society to the salary of the first AONB officer just appointed.

Last, he reported that task groups would be set up to undertake the routine duties contin-gent upon the Plan's effective functioning. This would allow the Technical Panel to operate a more general management role. In future the organisation would be known as the **Chiltern Conference**.

The Plan was the subject of considerable discussion following Harry Cook's statement. Tony Emery, the Society's Planning Adviser confirmed the appointment of Stephen Rodrick as the first AONB officer. This was the end of a long road that had been travelled since the idea of a body with appropriate staffing had been tentatively mooted in the late Sixties.

Forward Planning: a Society review for action

Harry Cook considered that the Executive Council often became disarrayed in its conduct of business, and decided to approach this matter through a specially convened meeting at his home. In preparation he analysed the problem as he saw it, and circulated a paper (AUDIT '92) with the invitation. Explaining his purpose to the subsequent Annual meeting he said:

"... the views expressed in the paper were entirely my own and what is more they were pretty critical and at times unfair to individuals on my hard working EC. I decided that the best thing would be to hold an informal discussion on AUDIT 92 ... at my home ... for a general talk and a snack luncheon, having issued the paper to each member of the EC."

"The reason for having the meeting at my home was because it is very, very difficult to lose your temper, storm out of the room, or have a furious argument if all this takes place at the Chairman's home where you are about to be given quite a pleasant little lunch."

"As the result of an amicable discussion we decided the best way to handle AUDIT '92 would be to ... form a Forward Planning Committee to address the issues."

The Committee, led by Edward Newmark produced a five-point plan entitled *A Strategy for Development*:

- to strengthen the ability of the Society to protect the interest of the area over which it operates;
- to obtain for the whole area of the Hills a stronger planning protection than is currently provided

by the existing AONB and Green Belt designation;
- to develop and progressively strengthen a working relationship within the Chiltern Conference ;
- to develop the internal activities of the Society and,
- to organise a Society to achieve these aims."

There were three main proposals:

First, to create a General Purposes Committee to handle routine business which tended to overload the agenda of the Executive Council making efficient functioning difficult;

second, to organise three regional meetings each year in, respectively, the north, mid and south Chilterns (one in each location);

third, to separate the roles of EC Vice Chairman from that of Group Chairman, to enable the Vice Chairmen to oversee particular blocks of the Society's business, policy development or interests and to free them to deputise for the Chairman as needed. The holding of both Group chairmanship, and Society vice chair simultaneously was barred. (CN.129)

These proposals caused lively discussion at the Annual General Meeting; most comment was positive. However, some members were sceptical about the intended regional meetings. Archie Campbell pointed out that the idea had been tried with very marginal results during his time in office. Initially successful, attendance had dwindled after the first year. There was also the further issue of the extra time demands upon the Executive Council's officers.

Edward Newmark explained that regional meetings were intended to enable more members to play an active and more democratic part in the Society's business. The proposal would have a year's trial; if it failed the scheme would be discontinued. The proposal to bar Group Chairmen from dual office holding was also positive. The Committee believed that this would encourage a sharper focus upon each Group to report at Council meetings. It would allow the Society's Vice Chairmen to concentrate upon EC matters and to deputise for the Chairman.

Supporting the proposals, John Memery, a Vice Chairman and former Treasurer, considered them an important step forward. He recalled one Executive Council when Matters Arising had taken an hour and a half to clear before the main business began. This was an inefficient and undesirable state of affairs.

The report was agreed for a year's trial. The number of EC meetings annually was reduced from ten to six to ease the pressure upon officers, and to facilitate sub-committee meetings. The proposal for a General Purposes Committee was not fully implemented, but developed in the more convenient form of an Officers' Meeting.

Appointment policy - Public Relations

In a separate discussion it was agreed by the AGM, on the Chairman's strong recommendation, to seek a professionally qualified Public Relations Officer. This would be a volunteer, recently retired from the profession or someone with sufficient experience and able to devote the time. He believed that the person appointed to this task should have no other commitments in the Society.

Pam Hawken, who had been PRO together with other responsibilities since 1982, agreed to stand down, and seek election to the Executive Council as a members' representative. In this manner she would be able to continue her work for the Society. Derek Whitson, a retired professional public relations executive was elected.

A moment of redirection for the Chiltern Society?

Considered in retrospect the Annual General Meeting of 1993 was a watershed in the development of the Chiltern Society. Captain Harry Cook had planned to stand down in 1992, but his potential successor finding that she was unable to devote the time to the needs of the office, he agreed to continue for a further year. The outcome was his opportunity and capacity to carry through the reform of the Executive Council's procedures begun with AUDIT '92.

Harry Cook's other achievements in office were also as significant for the continued work of the Society. He raised the public profile of the organisation; he reviewed its finances and stabilised the administration. He fostered membership growth, bringing in Edward Newmark as Membership Secretary, and encouraged his plans for postal circulation and consequent increased membership

Harry sought to create member groups as a means of strengthening the local connections of the Society; in this he achieved some positive outcomes. Arguably his greatest success was the strengthening of links with the Chiltern Conference and the Society's intricate involvement in the creation of *The New Plan for the Chilterns 1994*. Harry Cook was elected a Vice President on retiring from the Chairmanship.

Christopher Tatham, the General Secretary stood down at the time of Harry's departure, having given notice the year before on health grounds. He had served the Society since 1987, bringing to the work stability and administrative efficiency that was needed following a period of discontinuity in the role. Pressures of business, unanticipated job offers, and a lack of personal time had inhibited his immediate predecessors.

Christopher brought a stronger, firmer order to the job despite a serious illness soon after he was elected. He worked quietly and surely to ensure that Harry Cook's reforms received the administrative support essential to their ultimate success, and was aided in administration first by Christine Adnitt, the existing Assistant General Secretary, and then by Christine Preston who was appointed in 1990, later changing the title to Administrator.

The incoming Chairman, in October 1993, was Dr Barry Scott. He was still a practising consultant in the minerals field, and as a resident of South Bucks, was familiar with major issues concerning the Society in that area: Terminal 5 at Heathrow, the proposal by the Central Railway, plans for widening the M25, together with those for a service station on the M40, combined with the unfolding of the penultimate stages of the Misbourne campaign.

The new Vice Chairmen were John Memery (former Treasurer) and Peter Mansell-Moullin (previously Minerals Adviser). Each was pioneering the new role for vice chairman predicated by the recent AGM decision. Peter Mansell-Moullin resigned after one year on moving to Scotland; his successor was Michael Rush from the Water Resources Group.

PROJECTS OF THE TIMES

Bottom Wood, an ancient woodland

Bottom Wood proved a remarkable site. Mrs Cynthia Ercolani, appointed a Vice President, maintained a keen interest in the work of continuing her development of the Wood as a nature reserve. John Stidworthy, who chaired the Bottom Wood Group, and its predecessor Trees and Woodlands Group, traced the original probable ownership to the Abbey of Fontrevault in the Loire Valley. In 1413, following the suppression of foreign monastries, the land became Crown property. John wrote:

"Almost certainly there has been woodland on this ground for many hundreds of years, if not always. Plants in the wood include many indicators of ancient woodland, such as wood spurge, yellow archangel, wood sorrel, sweet woodruff, bluebell, goldilocks and primrose. The only sign that any farming ever took place in the wood is near the western end where, on the slope opposite the old well, there are terraces. They may have been strip fields in Saxon or even earlier times."

The Wood provides a fascinating insight into the rural industrial craft past of the Chiltern beech woods. In his short book, *History in the Chiltern Woodlands* John Morris sketch plots the archaeological sites extant in Bottom Wood. There are ancient lynchet banks, sawpits where the sawmen – top-dog and under-dog – worked in hazardous conditions to produce the boards and planks for buildings and manufacture. One can only wonder what, for example, was the effect on the lungs and eyes of the underdog deep in the pit and sawing upwards. John Morris identifies old trackways used to transfer the sawn articles out of the wood, a well to provide a water supply for the workers, and the probable remains of a charcoal maker's hearth. Each and all these are indicative of Bottom Wood as a site previously supporting the traditional woodland work of the Chilterns.

Most of the mammals that you would expect to find in a southern English woodland, from badger and fox down to wood mouse and pigmy shrew have been seen there. Rather less expected were the red deer that spent two days in the wood one Christmas, the polecats that bred a few years ago and the water shrew that are sometimes seen. A feature of the wood is the conservation programme for the common dormice, for whom devoted Society members have made the requisite nesting boxes to precise measurements.

Woodland birds make good use of the Wood. Tree creepers, nuthatches and species of woodpecker have been recorded. Species of tit including the marsh tit may be seen In the autumn, feeding on the berries of spindle trees. Red kites are often seen flying overhead; tawny owls and sparrow hawks breed regularly within the precincts.

Amphibians include plenty of frogs and toads, although there is no body of water in or close to the wood. The common newt has been recorded, but no reptile. Insects abound: butterflies, beetles, crickets, dragonflies, red-tailed bumble bees, wood wasps and parasites. On warm summer evenings the bright tails of female glow-worms can be clearly seen. This habitat is set in a landscape where adjacent fields still bear the names they had before the English Civil War.

The gift encouraged a different focus to the Society and the Trees and Woodlands Group. It was the first property to be wholly owned by the organisation and this fact brought a new responsibility. They owned it; it belonged to them; it was theirs for as long as they remained capable of its management and care. If, at some future time this task becomes impossible then the Wood must be gifted to another organisation able to continue the duty. This remains a critical requirement.

To Rescue a River, the Misbourne and Chalfont Lake (1982-2000)

During the early Eighties Vic Wotton joined the Water Resources Group (WRG), to become its secretary later, and the Chiltern Society, in search of help to resolve the Misbourne problem. From being a strong, fast flowing river in the 18th Century, it had dwindled so that for only brief periods each year, it continued to flow beyond Amersham. Vic believed he knew the answer but needed support to test and promote his theory.

The WRG Chairman was Bernard Banfield, founding member of the Society and water resources enthusiast. He had a dream of re-watering the Wendover Arm of the Grand Union Canal, and was alert also to the problems of many chalk streams flowing north from the scarp and south from the dip-slope. The two men joined forces, writing to Thames Water in 1983, seeking information about the amount of water taken from the river each year.

"Vic believed that, not withstanding other factors contributing to the failure of the river, the major cause was the excessive abstraction of water by the Company." (Vol.III p.25)

Vic also had a concern, shared by Harry Cook, about the deteriorating condition of Chalfont Lake, and considered that the failure of the Misbourne was part of that problem too.

By the mid-Eighties progress was being made; meetings with the Colne Valley Park Authority, Bucks County Council and Thames Water were producing official interest and some results. Thames Water had given a promise to undertake the re-watering of the Lake. Colne Valley had offered help with the Misbourne which joins the Colne at Denham, and Shell Petroleum were prepared to pay for replacement sluice gates on the river. Vic Wotton and the Chiltern Society had organised and started its campaign **To Rescue a River**.

In January 1987, Vic wrote and published, with Society backing, his extensive, detailed and authoritative analysis of the Misbourne problem, under this campaign title. The book illustrates the river's beauty in Victorian, Edwardian and early twentieth century years, when 11 mills were powered over its 17 miles' length. Chalfont Lake was one of its glories, and was home to many species of wild life and fish. Writing the foreword to the book, Derek Martin, Society Chairman, says:

"It is a definitive account of considerable research over a period of about ten years, supported by written and visual evidence, of how an attractive feature of the countryside – only about 30 miles from London – has been damaged by legalised over-abstraction and environmental neglect."

He concludes:

"It is pleasant to record that the organisation now responsible for the river, Thames Water Authority who inherited, but did not create the present situation, have already made a start at restoring the Chalfont Park Lake."

Vic's campaign received wide-ranging support, from the Chilterns, elsewhere in the United Kingdom, and overseas. His second book, *Misbourne Miscellany*, also highlighted the river's history in pictures, and its importance as a Chilterns chalk stream.

In December 1986 Thames Water commissioned Sir William Halcrow and Partners to prepare a survey of the Misbourne with a view to its possible restoration. Their first report confirmed Vic Wotton's opinions and research.

The Halcrow Consultancy final report was made in the spring of 1988, and Thames Water stated their intention to go ahead with the programme. It was the largest environmental scheme entered into by Thames Water and would ease the problem of extracting water from the Misbourne. But:

"… in 1988, drought conditions caused the water to retreat as in earlier years, … expectations were high that all was about to be put right." (Vol III p.26).

During the spring of 1988 Don Millar and the Conservation Volunteers team, together with Ivor Brent and his team worked on weed and undergrowth clearance. When work finished, Don Millar organised a celebration barbeque at the Royal Oak's field, close to the work site, and invited Society members to see the results. The Misbourne had become visible for a considerable stretch from Suffolk Bridge.

Water privatisation, and the creation of the National Rivers Authority (NRA), in 1989, stalled further progress. The new Authority made an early investigation of rivers significantly diminished by abstraction; the Misbourne was on the list of the 20 worst affected rivers nationally. The issue during the subsequent four years was who should pay: Government, the water companies, or the consumer?

The Misbourne – Action at last!

Vic's successor as Group secretary was Michael Rush. In 1993/94 the campaign was restarted and contact made with both the Office of the Water Services (OFWAT) and the Secretary of State for the Environment. Letters were sent to local MPs and residents; public meetings were arranged. Michael sought to mobilise help from the media, especially the local press, which printed articles and correspondence and provided useful support. The campaign succeeded. Michael Rush has written since:

"By '93 … Halcrow had done its report (1988); the problem of over-abstraction had been accepted and NRA had developed their preferred remedial work. We (WRG) then led a campaign to persuade OFWAT and the Government to include the project in the approved list for action by the water companies.

"We had tremendous support from local residents and local authority organisations, for a letter-writing campaign. … I well remember writing to the Secretary of State for the Environment … pointing out that the new Government could improve their green credentials at no cost to themselves (as the water companies were paying) by approving the scheme. Thankfully they did." (CS Archive letter. 12.01)

In 1994, an OFWAT decision that the water companies should finance remediation schemes (ALFS – the Alleviation of Low Flow Schemes) paved the way for the River Rescue, brokered by the NRA, to go ahead. Vic Wotton, now retired secretary of the WRG, was elected a Vice President of the Chiltern Society in recognition of his great achievements.

On 10 May 1995 a conference was held in Great Missenden, at which the National Rivers Authority, Thames Water, and Three Valleys Water presented their proposals. *Action at Last!* was the headline in the September *Chiltern News*. The companies and the NRA outlined their plans and described the way forward. Phase 1 would seek to re-water the Misbourne effectively; Phase 2 would provide a second, more extensive procedure if the first was not wholly successful. The News report ends:

"Michael Rush, on behalf of the Chiltern Society and as a local resident, warmly welcomed the positive commitment of the NRA and water companies to reduce abstraction from the Misbourne."

He was particularly glad that the work would be targetted at the upper end of the river, thus ensuring that the whole would benefit. He regretted that the NRA target for Phase 1 had slipped to April 1997. The Thames Water representative promised to review this.

In December 1996 John Norris, writing in *Chiltern News* discussed the progress that had been made. He recalled the recent Study Exchange visit to the Chilterns of eight environmental scientists. Three were from the USA, one from Canada, and four from the UK; they had been especially interested in the work to re-establish the Misbourne. John reported:

"Preliminary works are already in progress and on schedule but modification of existing pumping and pipeline facilities will be considerable and work will not be completed before the end of 1998."

In the event, this estimate proved pessimistic. Work was scheduled to be completed by March 31 1998 but all major works were finished by the beginning of the year. The article concluded;

"The forecast for the notoriously leaking section of the Misbourne downstream from Amersham is less clear-cut. If it is observed that flows there are still inadequate then Phase 2 of the plan will be implemented." (CN.No.142.)

Earlier in the year Three Valleys Water had organised a meeting at Chalfont St Peter to publicise plans and progress aimed at easing the flow below Amersham. A pipeline was under construction from West Hyde, near Rickmansworth to Chalfont St. Giles that would meet the public demand for water hitherto abstracted from the Misbourne. Don Brooks, reporting on this meeting, said:

"The seal was finally set on the proceedings when Vic Wotton appeared with a spring in his step and a broad smile. We knew then that something was really happening." (CN.144.)

John Norris completed the record in the September 1998 issue of *Chiltern News*, and raised an important question about the future.

"At the time of a desperately dry February (1998), it began to appear that this winter's aquifer recharge was about to run out of steam, and that the new abstraction regime would be starting with spring water tables lower than at any time since 1992. April changed all that. The rains that brought distress and havoc to some parts of England were a boon to the Chilterns, and initiated strong groundwater recovery which, unusually, continues in mid-June.

"The summer regime of increased evapotranspiration should soon reverse this trend, but the recovery so far, together with reduced abstractions in the months ahead, must augur well for the chances of improved flow next winter. The biggest remaining question mark concerns the flow through the Chalfonts. The section of the river after Amersham to Chalfont Park is a 'losing stream' with leakage through the river bed exceeding gains from surface springs; further intervention may yet be required to restore reasonably regular flow to this section." John adds:

Food for thought

"For once to everyone's satisfaction we should be well pleased with the outcome of a crusade started 20 years ago by Vic Wotton, and supported vigorously by the Society, but whilst celebrating the past we should also cast an eye to the future. With demand for water forecast to rise by 20% by 2020 the struggle to achieve a sustainable balance between environmental needs and management of supplies looks set to run and run. The Misbourne is just the tip of the iceberg; all our chalk streams will become increasingly at risk. Is it not time to bite the bullet and give serious consideration to other means, such as regional transfers to augment the public water supply in lowland Britain?" (CN.Vol 149.)

PART FOUR

The situation in 1993/94

Dr Barry Scott was elected Chairman in October 1993. He had been Society Roads Adviser, and he represented them on the Technical Panel of the Chiltern Conference. These responsibilities, together with his professional qualifications and expertise gave him an insight into some of the immediate current planning issues that concerned Chiltern Society members.

There were proposals for widening the M25 to four lanes over much of its northern and easterly route. There was an intention to site a Motorway Service Area near Iver in South Bucks; the Central Railway study presaged a freight transfer depot at Denham; in addition, the complex Public Inquiry into the proposed Terminal 5 at Heathrow Airport claimed the Society's planning Advisers and leading Officers' constant attention. In the broad perspective of the Chilterns it was important that the Society developed a new relationship with the Chiltern Conference and constructively assist the formulation of its proposed *Management Plan for the Chilterns*, then in the final stages. That was for the future; more urgently the Society's Planning Team's quality and strength were needed to tackle the wide variety of planning issues for the area, which were rising to greater prominence in the early Nineties.

SOME PLANNING PROBLEMS OF THE PERIOD

Pitstone Hill – a continuing planning problem (1993-2001)

Pitstone Cement Works had been a prime issue since the foundation of the Chiltern Society. The works closed finally in 1991, but in 1994 Castle Cement Company proposed to use one of the quarries as a household waste landfill site

For the Society this new application was a further turn of the screw. Closure of the cement works had not led to relief for the villages at the foot of Pitstone Hill; it appeared to many local residents that the battle for restoration was beginning again. The *Chiltern News* report, written by Geoffrey Legge and Bernard Banfield, campaigned under the slogan:

Pitstone Hill ... no thanks! NO DUMP!

Collaborating closely with local residents, who had formed the Beacon Hills Society, a powerful lobby and demonstration was mounted when councillors from Bucks and Hertfordshire visited the site. The Society's Chairman, and its Planning Adviser, submitted a very strong case to both local authorities for refusing planning permission.They:

"emphatically objected to (both) Bucks and Herts County Councils about the Company's quarry and transport proposals" (CN.133)

They pointed out the great advantages of natural self-restoration and informed all other principal bodies of the Society's objections and stance. Bucks and Herts Councillors unanimously rejected the Company's proposals, and the Secretary of State refused the appeal after a 38-day Inquiry.

By 1998 the works demolition was well advanced, and the following year a master plan for the site was approved. Peter Youngman, Geoffrey Larminie and Geoffrey Legge worked steadily to secure a sensible solution to the redundant quarries although negotiation with Castle Cement proved difficult. Proposals were presented for 650 houses and a commercial area; the Company sold all their sites to a developer; an agreement was made for the continuing extraction of chalk for agricultural use and a positive future of Quarry 3 as College Lake Nature Reserve was secured.

The Central Railway freight proposals

In 1990 the Central Railway Company was established to study the feasibility of, and make appropriate proposals for, a freight transit line from Glasgow in the north to Paris, Vienna and Milan. The plan eventually presented to Parliament proposed using the West and East Coast main lines, with a spur line to a collecting depot at Denham, at the southern tip of the Chilterns.

The Society was not opposed to the principle of the scheme; its policy was to encourage proposals which removed heavy freight traffic from road to rail. Peter Cleasby, Transport Adviser presented both positive and negative aspects of the published plan to the Executive Council, so far as these affected the Society's area of interest. The proposals could reduce the numbers of heavy lorries passing through the Chilterns; equally train traffic would become more intensive on the West Coast line.

Society Chairman Barry Scott wrote to the Secretary of State detailing the Society's concerns. Government turned down the scheme as presented on grounds of insufficiency of financial support, and the need for more detailed technical study and information. Meanwhile Central Rail had improved their organisational structure, sought stronger financial backing, and in 1995, had acquired PLC status.

During 1996 and 1997 a new set of proposals was prepared, designed to use the southward course of the old Great Central Railway, with modifications where this, over time, had been developed for housing or industrial use. The eventual track would run part of its way parallel with the Chiltern Line although Chiltern Rail expressed reservations.

In 1998 the revised plan was presented to Parliament. The Chiltern Society was advised by Walter Horn (now Transport Adviser) that the proposal was an improvement on the previous scheme. However, in Buckinghamshire the Central Railway Action Group (CRAG) renewed its alert. David Lidington, MP for Aylesbury Vale and a Shadow Minister for the Environment spoke against the Plan at a meeting organised by the residents of Longwick village, south of Thame. He said there were substantial obstacles to the Company's goal. His subsequent correspondence with the Rail Regulator, with Railtrack, and local MPs (copied to the Chiltern Society) confirmed his opinion. Parliament voted against the scheme.

At the end of 2000, Central Railway proposed to present a Bill during the next Parliamentary Session. In a change of tactic, early in 2001, the Company announced its intention to seek from the Secretary of State a hybrid Bill which, if granted, would by-pass some of the normal planning procedures. Mark Januszewski (Planning Group Secretary) noted in *Chiltern News* that the Government had indicated it would not:

> "... take a position until the Strategic Railway Authority (SRA) had concluded a review of the economic and technical implications of the proposal - which could take a number of years."
> (CN.160.p18)

The Consultant to the SRA made a confidential report to the Authority; at the start of 2003 they were continuing to study the matter. The Society continues to hold a watching brief.

AIRPORTS IN THE CHILTERN SOCIETY'S AREA OF INTEREST

Two major airports (London Heathrow and London Luton) caused much concern to the Society during the 1990s.

London Heathrow and Terminal 5 (T5)

This was a great planning shadow for nine years from 1993 to 2002. The Society made numerous submissions to the Public Inquiry, both verbal and written and Francis Cory-Wright, Airports Adviser, Tony Emery and other Planning personnel and Advisers, attended many of the hearings during that time.

A submission in December 1993 by Walter Horn and the Chairman, Barry Scott, made many prime points that were to receive constant attention during the subsequent years. Their submission brought strong support from Society members, and included reference to the plans for a large area of shopping services, and the likely consequential increase in road traffic. They argued that reasonable alternatives had not been considered, that there was no national transport policy, that little thought had been given to passenger numbers, and insufficient attention had been given to the economics and impact of proposed retail developments.

Both Barry and Walter believed debilitating disruption of road systems would occur, and pollution and noise would damage the environment. Heathrow had already reached saturation point and the key to Europe was rail, not air. Further:

"the published figures also suggest, airside and landside, **Terminal Five is to become another superstore rather than a terminal**, resulting in increased traffic movements arising from increased staff in the retail facilities."

Francis Cory-Wright representing the Society at the subsequent Public Inquiry in May 1995 reinforced these points, and numerous others. He summarised the main points at issue, re-stating also that the Chiltern Society believed future airport development should be off-shore on reclaimed land where less environmental damage would occur. The Society's sub-mission was re-written to address the matter from the standpoint of the five main focus points in line with which the Inquiry was now organised. These were:

- Description and Justification of proposals in terms of Air Transport.
- Development Pressures and Socio-Economic Impacts (including Regional and Sub-Regional Planning Context).
- Land Use Policy.
- Surface Access (including impact upon the Present and Committed Road Network).
- Air Quality.

In his concluding set of observations, presented early in 1999, Francis made three very strong points for the Inspector's consideration:

"there is (no) such thing as 'poor quality' Green Belt, an observation made by the developer greedy to take part of the Colne Valley Park. There is 'neglected' Green Belt…(but)…it has been pointed out that new legislation envisages landowners being required to put right their neglected Green Belt land."

He strongly emphasised also that:

"… any further intrusion by Heathrow into the Green Belt is the thin edge of the wedge, encouraging new and additional sources of traffic congestion, ultimately leading to the related proliferation of other applications to develop 'poor quality' Green Belt areas."

Francis' final thrust was to give the Inspectors an urgent reminder of why the Green Belt was created and what it is for. (CN.151.)

In a letter to Cic Upcott (January 2002), he notes that:

"because of the length of time it took, and the enormous cost of the Inquiry (c£53 million), … one certain consequence … is an overhaul of the entire planning regimen, whereby future national or regional plans on this scale will be committed to Parliamentary scrutiny in the first instance to decide the issues in principle; accordingly the democratic dimension as it currently prevails will revert to the Lords and Commons."

In 2002, despite the strong opposition from environmental groups, County and District

Councils and London Boroughs, and many civic organisations, Government decided to proceed with Terminal 5.

London Luton Airport (LLA)

A meeting in November 1998, convened at the Society's request, considered the progressive expansion of LLA. In summing up the meeting, Chairman Michael Rush pointed out that the airport was bidding to be a major London terminal, and seeking the advantage of a closer position to London than either Gatwick or Stansted. This was a long way from its original function as a small municipal airport. (CN.151)

More recently Francis Cory-Wright has reported that the forecast and approved passenger numbers passing through Luton have been significantly exceeded. An initial figure of 3 million passengers per annum (3 mppa) had risen to an estimated 6 mppa and possibly more. The increase occurred in part because of extensive use by two 'low-cost' airlines. Another forecast suggests a potential of between 10 mppa and 30 mppa.

A matter of further anxiety is the continued absence of an effective rail link; passengers have to detrain at Luton Parkway, and bus into the main terminal.

The Society's prime concern is one of flight patterns that could cause more noise pollution to residents. It was pointed out that the Bedfordshire Structure Plans had envisaged a 10 mppa target; that had undoubtedly influenced the Government's own forward forecast. The Society also supported the campaign for lower noise (decibel) levels, seeking a return to a modified 1984 structure, and advocating a thoughtful spreading of flight patterns to keep noise intrusion to a minimum level.

In summarising the 1998 Conference Michael Rush pointed to the difficulty in adopting an absolute position with regard to further expansion of Luton Airport, and argued for a balanced view: He said:

"... It cannot reasonably be argued that the airport enterprise is not an asset for those living and working in the Chilterns and who wish to use its facilities from time to time; the opportunity for cheap and convenient air travel is not, of course, confined to passengers coming from London but is also welcomed by those living closer to the airport. It remains the case, however, that it is these very factors that the Chiltern Society and other amenity organisations have to contend with, unfortunately." (CN.151)

At the end of 2002, the issue for the Society remained one of careful watch on developments, attempting to moderate the pace of expansion that, it believed, could do much harm to the area of the north Chilterns should it become too rapid.

Housing and urban development

Between 1994 and 2001 many housing plans were being drawn to the Society's attention as matters of concern. Proposed developments in Wycombe, at Hemel Hempstead and

Stevenage caused great public alarm. Submissions to the planning authorities were made by the Society on its own behalf; it also supported other groups making similar protests including the Hertfordshire Society (CPRE).

THE PLANNING TEAM

From 1991 until 1997, Dr Tony Emery was Planning Adviser, and members included Geoffrey Legge, who later headed the Team as Planning Co-ordinator. Other key participants were David Lindsey, Barbara Wallis, and Tad Effendowicz, who made particular contributions to the campaign for reduced speed limits on country roads. Geoffrey Larminie, widely experienced expert geologist who became Geological and Environmental Adviser, Francis Cory-Wright the Airports Adviser, Walter Horn, Transport Adviser and Peter Youngman, Landscape Adviser, completed the lead group. In support were a Chiltern-wide team of 24 to 26 volunteer Field Planning Officers covering all local Districts and Boroughs.

In December 2001 the Group Secretary was Mark Januszewski, who also managed Specialist Group contact and liaison with the Field Planning Officers and 16 Assistants. Other specialist Advisers included Hugh Norwood and Jane Griffin (Planning procedures and documents), and Reg Free (London Green Belt). Geoffrey Legge (Planning Co-Ordinator) had the extra roles of a Planning Field Officer and representative of the Chiltern Society on the Planning Committee of the Shadow Chilterns Conservation Board, which the Chiltern Conference had now become.

A Steering Committee to review policy and progress met quarterly. Action was initiated "where they had clout", and were therefore likely to be most effective. Geoffrey Legge commented that, in 1998, Government alone had issued some 150 consultative papers within the 12-month period. He added: "Fortunately not all affecting us!"

By January 2001, the Group activity had reached 8,000 hours annually, studying around 3,000 planning applications in the year, and responding as necessary.

Co-ordinating Planning Team restructuring

The Planning Team had been re-organised early in 1997. Contact between the Specialist Groups and the Planning Team existed informally through membership of the Executive Council. Joint action upon issues occurred where liaison was obviously necessary. Geoffrey Legge proposed an improved modus operandi redefining the Planning Team's functions and providing for improved liaison and collaboration with all Groups across the Society. His Report to the Executive Council said:

"**County Teams**

"County and District based teams will deal with all planning matters in their area. Planning Field Officers will continue to deal with basic matters.

"Major issues:

"County and District plans, bypasses etc, will be considered at meetings called by Team convenors as necessary. Delegates from Chiltern Society Groups will be asked to join these meetings. Sub-committees including planning advisers will consider Government consultation papers.

"Planning Advisers

"(These are) ...Members with expertise in various fields, eg planning procedures, science, engineering, DoE papers, and landscape in the Green Belt, (who) have agreed to be consulted as necessary to ensure that professional responses can be made on major issues.

"Society Advisers

"The Planning Team will work closely with them on matters involving farming, airports, transport & roads, geology & environment, minerals & waste."

Lead Team activity included major matters such as proposed new super stores, motorway services areas, Castle Cement (Pitstone), Field Studies Centres and the like. Other issues requiring closer scrutiny such as housing developments which threatened the environment, the use of greenfield sites, footpath diversion, increasing road traffic, the relative adequacy of Council services, and many others, made inter-Group contact and co-ordination ever more critical. Since 1998 the creation of Regional Development Agencies (RDAs) endowed with some major planning powers and Government financing has strengthened that necessity.

The changes were welcomed and seen as a positive response to the growing understanding of inter-dependence in environmental problems; more regular inter-Group liaison had become essential. With the addition of Planning Assistants working to the Planning Advisers, the operating structure introduced in 1997/98 is the one used continuously since that time

GOVERNMENT PROPOSALS AFFECTING THE CHILTERN ENVIRONMENT

SERPLAN: (Sustainable Development Strategy for the South-East)

In 1998 the Planning Team responded to the Government's consultation paper, which proposed some 9,000 houses for the Chilterns and 1.7 million for the country, with a rising density per hectare, up to the year 2008. The use of Green Belt land was regarded as essential.

The Planning Team's response advocated an external audit of brownfield sites, guidance on hectare density, and no weakening of the London Green Belt. They wanted the AONB kept outside regional housing development plans. The housing numbers forecast was considered "in excess of foreseeable requirements".

The Team also wanted measures to assist economic regeneration but sought strong control over commercial development. They strongly opposed Terminal 5 at Heathrow because of commercial pressures this would produce, and the consequent greater traffic congestion, noise and atmospheric pollution. They urged tighter regulation of Luton airport development. Other points in the response were the need for reduced speed limits on country roads, planning security for definitive paths and rights of way, and greater protection for the Chiltern woodlands.

Finally, they proposed mandatory water metering, consultation with the Environment Agency about water supply before new housing was authorised, and that ground water extraction should be realistically regulated especially in chalk stream countryside. A revised draft SERPLAN included many of the points made in the Society's response, in common with those of other organisations.

After receiving responses to the second draft, Government consultants reviewed the proposals. The subsequent Crowe Report was widely and heavily criticised for returning to many of the original, unacceptable draft proposals. A final draft SERPLAN was published in March 2001.

Geoffrey Legge and Mark Januszweski commented:

"This 110-page document is, except in one respect, a final draft, the only matter for further consultation being housing number distribution between the counties. The DETR want 39,000 houses per year to be built "on the footprint of 33,000", in other words at greater densities than previously proposed." After 2006 … "it is believed a rate of 43,000 will be required." (CN.157)

However housing allocations for the four AONB counties were better than previous proposed figures and there was

"a reworded policy on the Green Belt, improvements in the water policies to protect quality and supply and to avoid building on flood plains…a policy on improved access to the countryside includes more emphasis on walking and cycling." (CN.157)

The Rural White Paper (Our Countryside - A Fair Deal for Rural England)
This White Paper was forecast during the 2001 Foot and Mouth epidemic. Its purpose was to review many aspects of rural life and the economy, and the proposals held many implications for the Chilterns and the AONB. It was published before Christmas 2000; the Planning Team's note to Chiltern News said that:

" there is much to be welcomed in this 175-page document which includes the following undertakings." (CN 159.)
- A Cabinet Committee on Rural Affairs
- Rural 'proofing' of government policies
- A Charter for country matters
- A Community Service Board operated by the Countryside Agency to 'protect' rural parks, post

offices, shops and village facilities.

- A Rural Development Plan for Agriculture
- Rural housing enablers based on Countryside Agency sector scheme.
- Social housing grants for affordable housing
- A £4.5 million fund to improve countryside around towns
- To achieve Conservation Board status for 'Four large AONBs by 2004'.
- Stronger planning protection for AONBs
- Transport funding including

> £132 million for rural bus subsidies,
>
> £60 million for rural bus 'challenge';
>
> £15 million Parish fund for transport issues, to be operated by the Countryside Agency,
>
> 'Quality Parishes' for local solutions,
>
> Improved access to the country through the Countryside Bill,
>
> A green spaces initiative.

The Planning Team

"... is studying the implications and is consulting with the Countryside Agency, Chilterns Conference (Shadow Board), Civic Trust and others."

Geoffrey Larminie, Chairman then of the Farming Liaison Group, Geological and Environmental Adviser to the Society, took a different view. He found the White Paper flawed and argued that:

"(it is)...littered with visions of a pastoral world that has long ceased to exist and is short on commitment to an integrated plan for the whole fabric of Britain, rural and urban."

By mid-year 2003, legislation to give effect to the proposals had yet to be proposed.

Regional Development and Regional Assemblies – carts before horses ?

The Planning and Compulsory Purchase Bill published in December 2001 proposes regionalisation, and the virtual abolition of County Council planning powers. District Councils duties are to be reorganised. This very apparent threat to local democracy is causing great concern; the Society has made its views known to the Deputy Prime Minister and to the Chiltern MPs.

Regional Development Assemblies are currently nominated un-elected bodies. Government is consulting to ascertain whether the Regions wish to have elected bodies. In either case the Assemblies will be responsible for producing special planning strategies replacing the County Structure Plans. The problem for the Chiltern Society, from 2002 forwards, is the division of its area between two Regions and, ultimately if the process is followed, between two Assemblies' areas of responsibility. Bedfordshire and Hertfordshire are in the Eastern Region (provisionally based in Cambridge); the South-East Region includes

Buckinghamshire and Oxfordshire and is currently serviced from Government offices in Guildford.

This divided responsibility was sharply identified by Francis Cory-Wright, Airports Adviser to the Chiltern Society. In January 2002, he wrote:

"The arbitrary division of the Realm into Regions has led to the unexpected consequence of the Chilterns being cleft in twain. ... The result for airports is that we now have two different Government offices because Luton (and Stansted) is now in one Region and Heathrow in another."

The Chiltern Society, the Shadow Conservation Board, and many amenity groups have subsequently proposed a sub-regional status for the AONB in order to maintain a unified approach to planning policy. The proposals as a whole supersede many of those in SERPLAN, and some of the structures outlined in the Rural White Paper. Further Government consultation is expected in 2003.

THE CHILTERN CONFERENCE (shadow Chilterns Conservation Board)

Management Planning for the Chilterns

During Captain Harry Cook's Chairmanship, the Chiltern Conference had grown in stature and influence. The Society had representation on its working groups and main committee. In 1994 the Conference published its *Management Plan for the Chilterns* bringing AONB planning into sharper focus. The Society's Executive Council welcomed the Plan, and considered it had many constructive features. They expressed some concern at its limitation to the designated AONB boundaries but accepted the Plan in principle, and urged members to support it.

In an official response they pressed that the recently appointed AONB Officer, Steve Rodrick should have other staff in support as soon as this became practicable, and that his role should be to co-ordinate services provided by local councils rather than create new services. The Society agreed to contribute funds towards the Officer's salary, much welcomed at the time by Michael Gwilliam, the Bedfordshire Chief Planning Officer who chaired the Conference. In 2001 this amounted to £5,000 per annum. (By summer 2003, another eight staff members were in post. [*Chalk and Trees. Summer/Autumn 2003*])

Both bodies appreciated the advantages of co-operative working that they had achieved through long association since the first Plan in 1971. Michael Rush came to office in the Society, as Vice Chairman in 1995, during the Conference's development of its new Plan. He took great interest in fostering collaboration between the two organisations and contributed to many aspects of the Conference's work. On becoming Society Chairman in 1997 he continued to chart firmly the direction for joint working and association on projects of mutual interest, where an independent voice was constructive and valuable. He worked steadily to achieve this end representing the Society on what, by then, had become the Shadow Chilterns Conservation Board, until 2002, when he was succeeded by Robin Rowland. His influence had been significant and positive for the Society's future relationship with the new Board.

In 1996 Steve Rodrick wrote in *Chiltern News* about progress made in implementing the Plan. Headed *What's Going On* he set out a resume of the first year's achievements.

"three special Task Groups have been set up, Land Management, Planning, Recreation, Access and Tourism. Each Group has 10 to 12 members, and the Chiltern Society is represented on all of them."

The Land Management Group had four projects: first, the case for Environmentally Sensitive Area status; second, a completed survey of over 400 woodland owners; third, opposition to a proposed golf course at Penn Wood; fourth, a major workshop on agriculture and the planning system in the Chilterns AONB.

The Conference's Planning Group had commissioned a study on Chiltern building design. It strongly supported opposition to the Penn Wood golf course development; a major study about motor traffic on rural roads had started.

The Leisure, Access and Tourism Group was bidding for lottery money in preparation to provide a Chiltern-wide environmental information programme. It planned to host a conference on low flow alleviation based on the River Misbourne experience, for experts from the USA and the UK. There were plans for work on the river corridors of the Chess and the Misbourne.

HERITAGE, HISTORIC BUILDINGS AND CONSERVATION

The dangers to the environment of uncontrolled development and its potential effect upon the rural landscape, actively involved the minds and objectives of HWBG during the Nineties. Much of the environment seemed to be under threat.

Farm Buildings

In particular the Group was anxious to ensure the conservation of the Chiltern heritage of high quality traditional farm buildings, especially barns that were falling into disuse where contemporary farming methods often rendered the buildings redundant. An increasing number were being converted for housing and fostering a 'creeping urbanisation' in the rural landscape. In their efforts to moderate this process the Group was continuing the tradition of constructive engagement established in the Society's very earliest days.

In 1987 Laurence Evans, then Group Chairman, secured a resolution at the Society's AGM, enabling him to write to Chiltern local authorities proposing that each should establish a Conservation Area Local Advisory Committee. The purpose was to ensure more effective regulation and monitoring of changes to the use of buildings and the landscape.

Beautiful scenery is what the Chilterns is about, and the Society's major aim is to protect it – by caring for it physically, and by working to obtain better planning protection for it.

The problems faced in 1965 – *the M40, Pitstone Cement Works, and rubbish dumping.*

The challenges – *To save heritage buildings, like Lacey Green Windmill...*

...and to show how small woodlands could be looked after and people could be trained in their management, as in Bottom Wood. After clearance comes the replanting.

Another challenge: *To set up a site like Chiltern Open Air Museum, to which special buildings could be removed and re-erected for all to see and enjoy.*
TOP: *The Iron Age Hut being built by the Manshead Archaeological Society.*
BOTTOM LEFT: *Marsworth stable and cattleshed, and* RIGHT, *thatching Arborfield Barn, all from early days.*

Walking *was one of the first pursuits organized by the Society.* LEFT: *Walkers in Burnham Woods.* ABOVE: *Walking from Bix to Nettlebed.* BOTTOM LEFT: *Walkers from Northend, Henley, led by Dave Howarth.* BOTTOM RIGHT: *John Coombe shows Peter Illiffe the way(!), and the rest will follow.*

The Chiltern Way launch, October 2000.

ABOVE: *The walkers arrived at Coleshill, near Amersham, coming from two directions.*

LEFT: *Celebrating – it's official! From left to right: Michael Rush, (Chris Chillingworth), Chris Brasher, Cheryl Gillan, MP for Chesham and Amersham, Michael Meacher MP, Minister for the Environment, Sir John Johnson, Sir Leonard Figg.*

Water *is an important commodity, and the Chilterns has many beautiful streams and rivers, like the River Chess, here pictured in Hertfordshire* – RIGHT

BOTTOM LEFT: *The official sign that tells the world that the River Misbourne has been rescued.*
BOTTOM RIGHT: *RWCG carry out regular readings at boreholes on the Misbourne, the Bulbourne and the Gade in collaboration with the river authority.*

Conservation *comes in all forms.* ABOVE: *Re-exposing a large pudding stone at Stoke Row Hill in spring, 2000, with South Chiltern Volunteers.*

BELOW: *Clearing the banks of the Misbourne encourages water to run within the original course once more.*

Steps and Stiles –*The main work of the Path Maintenance Volunteers.*
ABOVE: *Reconstructing stiles is one of these guys' specialities, but whenever possible, kissing gates are being introduced now, or easier means of access.*

RIGHT: *Steps complete – and walkers are helped on their way up a steep bank.*

Ewelme Watercress Beds – *Another major rescue project.* ABOVE: *The bund restored; this is the central solid barrier that controls the water flow, and allows access.*

ABOVE LEFT: *Kingfishers, and many other flora and fauna return once more.*

RIGHT: *Unearthing the sluice of the one-time watermill.*

*The **Cyclegroup** has become a popular activity, with its weekly rides around the Chilterns.*

*The **SHOP** at Chesham Festival, 2000.*

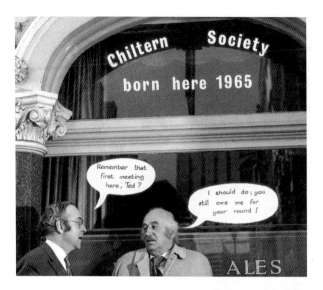

Celebrating – we're rather good at that.
Parties were held for the 10th, 21st, 25th, and 30th anniversaries.

LEFT: **Ten years old,** *and everything to go for! The two founders, Chris Hall and Ted Castle in a rare old photo montage.*

RIGHT: **At the 21st** *at Pipers Corner School, Christopher Hall cut the cake, left, and Wing Commander Derek Martin looked on.*

RIGHT – *An extra event: hundreds came to the* **Jubilee Picnic on Watlington Hill** *in 2002, where Jeremy Irons lit the beacon.*

The 25th was held at Fingest in a magnificent barn, with barbecue and entertainment following a walk, in wonderful weather.

BOTTOM: *The 30th was at the Rush's house, and the 220 odd members and friends had a marvelous time, again in glorious weather.*

More successes for the Chilterns – *the return of the Red Kite, much to everyone's pleasure.*

The splendidly personal demonstration at Pitstone against the retention of the Cement works, after much discussion and strong words about possible alternative plans for the site.

Few of the local authorities replied; a subsequent letter to the Secretary of State for the Environment suggesting changes in the law relating to Conservation Areas and Listed Buildings received no response. However, at the Annual Meeting in October 1990, Chairman Harry Cook praised the enterprise of the Group in its pursuit of a solution.

He reported that the Secretary of State had recently issued a Consultation Paper about planning permission for agricultural buildings. He had no doubt the Group would make an effective submission.

Building Watchers

In the early Nineties the HWBG also endeavoured to create a team of watchers to seek out and monitor individual buildings thought to be at risk. Considerable success was achieved; the Group's Annual Report for 1996 records visits to 23 potentially vulnerable buildings in the four counties. The Group's volunteers were very fully engaged throughout the year.

"(Each property was seen by)…one or more members of the Group's Committee or one of the Group's Conservation Watch Volunteers. Contacts were made or letters sent to the relevant Local Planning Authority or advice given to local residents who were concerned. A statement of objection was sent to the Planning Inspectorate in the case of Hall Place (Beaconsfield) which was the subject of a Public Inquiry." (Gp Annual Report, 1996)

Policy development and practice and regular meetings

From its inception in 1967 HWBG had met regularly each month except in December and August, constituting itself as an informal committee as needed. The customary pattern was to transact formal business (if required) followed by a talk, lecture, or discussion about issues of immediate interest or concern.

Pauline Wilkinson, its Secretary since 1984, became Chairman in 1994 and fostered a more structured approach to policies and process. During 1995 work she began to develop the Group's policy papers touching the topics of prime concern: ancient monuments, listed buildings, conservation areas, historic parks and gardens, traditional farm buildings, archaeological areas, and historic landscapes.

"An important aim was to finalise the 'policy papers' drafted during 1995, as a set of written documents to guide the work of the Group in a consistent way and to ensure that the Executive Council of the Chiltern Society were aware of our stance and broadly agreed with it." (Gp Annual Report 1996)

The HWBG also adopted a constitution to regulate its proceedings, and these were accepted by the Group, and finally endorsed by the Executive Council of the Chiltern Society on the 21 June 1996. The major revision of the Group's *Historic Farm Buildings and Farmsteads* policy document, formulated several years earlier, was continued and completed in 1997.

Programme enlargement

In the same period enlargement of the monthly programme was begun, and was further expanded in 1997 and 1998. The regular meetings were devoted to expert and specialist lectures, presentations and analysis of relevant topics. Speakers were invited from local amenity groups, local authorities, and national environmental organisations. The opportunity was taken to renew a link with the Chiltern Open Air Museum; Dick Amsden was Chairman of the HWBG when he launched the Museum in 1975.

The purpose of these new programmes was two-fold: firstly, to better inform members upon subjects connected with the group's policies, and secondly to increase contacts with like-minded organisations within the Chilterns. Usually, one meeting in six was devoted to formal business and the Annual General Meeting.

When Pauline Wilkinson succeeded to the Chair in 1996, Roger Gooding became Secretary and John Wellsman relinquished that task to devote more time to co-ordinating the (Buildings) Conservation Watch Volunteers. He continued to lead the Group's practical refurbishment of Bledlow Cross. Officers changed: Dr Marcia Bell replaced Roger Gooding after a time, Piers Harker was elected Vice Chairman and the meetings were supplemented by visits to buildings and places of historic interest. Harry McLean was Chairman in 1997/98. Pauline became Historic Buildings Adviser to the Society, remaining in that capacity into the new century. In September 1995, Group members led by Piers Harker visited Chalfont St Giles Conservation Area, and later in the year they went to the Pitstone Farm Museum. This visit was followed in 1998 by one to the Pitstone post mill; Jeff Hawkins, Society founder member and Vice President, whose father gave the mill to the National Trust, "treated us to half-an-hour's talk on the history of the windmill". Then followed a conducted tour led by David Lindsey, another Chiltern Society member, active at Ford End Watermill.

Resurgence and renewal

Harry McLean and Marcia Bell resigned during 1998 and Group momentum was lost for a time when, at the September AGM, a Chairman and a Secretary were needed. No nominations were received. Following an appeal in *Chiltern News* by Michael Rush, the Chiltern Society's Chairman, Christopher Wallis accepted the former role, with Tony Balfour taking on the secretarial duties and Betty Hardy providing further support. The Society's Annual Report in 1999 carried this appreciation from Michael:

"The Group (has) bounced back with renewed vigour and (has run) an excellent programme of monthly meetings and interesting visits to places of historic merit. This included a fascinating visit to Hampden House which is not normally open to the public, and I heartily congratulate the Group on their efforts."

Further evidence of this renewed vitality came one year later. Christopher Wallis reported that an Eyes and Ears sub-section had been started. Individual members undertook to watch buildings and territory, reporting unusual developments, or unexplained actions by owners.

A critical reappraisal and updating of the Group's 1995/96 *Barns and Farm Buildings* Policy was begun against the background of the continuing sale of Buckinghamshire County Council's farms. Concern was also expressed about the siting of CCTV masts in Marlow High Street, and the Group had given support to the Marlow Society's protests about the inadequacy of the related public consultation. Threats to a number of older Chiltern buildings had been identified; advice about the rebuilding of an ancient wall on the Misbourne in Amersham had resulted in the use of a Chiltern Society member's expertise and a much lower estimate of cost. The annual maintenance had been carried out on Bledlow Cross in cooperation with Central Chiltern Conservation Volunteers.

Barbara Wallis succeeded her husband as Chairman in September 2000; David Pamington continued with the Secretary's portfolio. The pattern of winter meetings and summer outings was sustained and strengthened.

Early in 2001 an important debate was arranged to discuss the motion, *"This Group believes that no traditional barn should be converted to housing"*. 24 people attended including the Conservation Officer for Wycombe District Council and a number of local farmers. The motion, proposed by Christopher Wallis and opposed by Reg Free, was lost. However the meeting accepted the need for conditions being imposed that would retain the historical character of the buildings and their settings. A follow-up meeting ratified the updated version of the HWBG's document *Policy for Historic Farm Buildings and Farmsteads in the Chilterns*.

Two talks about the use of traditional brick construction and wall pointing practice in the Chilterns were instructively and enjoyably enlarged by a visit to the local Matthew's Brickworks at Bellingdon. A third talk was given by Jenny Habib, Planning Field Officer for the Chiltern Society, who spoke about the newly established Building Design Awards jointly promoted by the Chilterns Conservation Board and the Society. The succeeding discussion revealed tensions evident in the debate on farm building conversions. Several members thought that these Awards tended to encourage conversion schemes.

Other talks included *The Romans in the Chilterns* given by Bambi Stainton, and another by Dr Rachel Brown in preparation for the Group's planned visit to Marlow. A new venture was the creation of a display stand at the annual meeting of the Bucks Local History Network.

Writing in the Society's Annual Report for 2000/01, Barbara Wallis stressed how well HWBG had revived and commented upon the debate, the talks' programme and the visits:

"All these meetings were successful and better attended than the previous year, thus contributing to the Chiltern Society's objective to inform and instruct its members."

In 2002 the talks and visits programme proved equally successful. A coup occurred in the form of a visit to *Halton House*, arranged by Betty Hardy. The house is the officers' mess for the RAF training unit established in 1918. Previously it was the country home of Baron Alfred Charles de Rothschild whose relatives owned other great houses in the region.

The mid-June visit to Hitchin followed a talk given earlier in the year by David Howlett, from the Hitchin Historical Society. The tour included the Corn Exchange, the Priory and the old British and Foreign Bible Society School now owned by a charitable Trust and housing a Museum of Education.

LACEY GREEN WINDMILL 1986-2003, a postscript by Christopher Wallis

Michael Hardy, the Group representative on the Executive Council was (and remains) the Honorary Secretary of the Lacey Green Windmill Committee.

From the summer of 1986 the mill has been open to visitors on Sunday afternoons from May to September, together with summer public holidays, the annual Lacey Green village day and National Mills Day. On these days we usually 'hoist the cloths' and let the sails turn, unloaded. On special occasions like Sheaf to Loaf Day we have ground some meal, which is inedible because it contains millstone grit (!) and the flour dresser isn't working yet.

Mills which have sails bent on to the sweeps (common sails) cannot be reefed without first stopping their rotation. If the wind suddenly increases violently, the handbrake windshaft will not be effective and the machinery will become uncontrollable until a part breaks, causing a (possibly) disastrous accident. The miller therefore has to be a captain of his 'sailing ship' and be able to judge the wind, so as to make alterations in good time. Dangerous work.

All structures have to be maintained against wear and weather, and Lacey Green windmill is no exception. The smock and sails are repainted every three to four years (a miller would do it every year). Michael Highfield greases the moving parts of the cap and its turning mechanism (the fan) and makes adjustments and minor repairs. Geoff Giles is paint master, and I maintain the woodwork and iron structural parts. Michael and Betty Hardy look after the static exhibition on the meal floor (basement), and organise the faithful group of volunteer wardens who attend every opening to look after visitors, collect entrance donations, and sell postcards, drawings and mugs.

The future looks good: we have recently started another 25-year lease from the owners, Rosemary and Nick Smith. We intend to set up our 8-mule Amanco oil engine to drive the Victorian barn mill and also mobile corn mill (wheelwright-built in 1867) on loan from the National Museum of Rural Life.

We learnt much while restoring the mill. Now we can interpret and pass this experience to the world at large.

FOOTPATH CONSERVATION AND RIGHTS OF WAY

The Rights of Way Group began several initiatives during the period after 1993. Led by John Rowe, and from autumn 1996 by John Coombe, with John Rowe stepping down to become Vice Chairman, the Group is the oldest constituent specialist Group of the Chiltern Society. Its major role following its foundation in early 1966 was to monitor and, with County Councils' approval carry out clearance and other maintenance on much of the Chiltern network of paths. This role has developed in recent times, responding to contemporary change, to include watch and care for bridleways.

By 2001 18 Area Secretaries and numerous footpath wardens carried out regular inspections to ensure access. This structure and function is pre-eminent of its kind among the Areas of Outstanding Natural Beauty. Barry Scott once described the Group's network as the best of its type in the country.

The traditions of long service and dedication begun by Don Gresswell, the Group's founder have been continued by many members. Among those having long involvement are Bill Chester (cartographer and map researcher until 1999 and sometime ROWG Secretary), Nick Moon (keen walker and member since the early 70s, writer, and planner of the Chiltern Way), Leslie Drain (Group Chairman 1986/90, and Area Secretary in South Oxfordshire for 30 years), the late Tony Emery (Group Chairman 1975/83), and the late Jean Jefcoate, member of the Ramblers' Association since the 1950s, and a leader in the opening up of the North Bucks Way. Later she joined the Chiltern Society as well, becoming Area Secretary for South Bucks (4b) from 1981 until her death in November 2000.

Many path representatives have served the ROWG for long periods including Christopher Lake, Stan Ward, Eileen Simmonds, Reg Greenaway, Malcolm Petyt and Ken Green. Different contributions were made by Ken Holdbrook as Newsletter aide, and assisting with the Sue Ryder walks programme; Brian Armstrong, Chairman of the ROWG in 1973/75 became the Society's Countryside Officer (part-time paid) c1988/90, returning to the Chair 1990/91 to be succeeded by John Rowe.

Policies and Practices

In 1993 the Group began a project to provide stiles suitable to be used by older people or those with less agility. John Rowe and Rob Bethell, the Group Secretary, visited centres of stile making; a trial model made by Tom Bindoff was bought and installed. A further Group policy urged owners and parish councils to replace stiles with kissing gates through which walkers can squeeze rather than climb. In collaboration with the Chiltern Conservation Volunteers, ROWG undertook a survey and reinstatement of decayed stiles. Since 1999 a review of unessential stiles is proposed to encourage owners to remove these barriers where they serve no useful function.

Close cooperation with local authority rights of way officers was frequently found to be the key which facilitated action to re-instate access to ploughed-over rights of way. For the regular maintenance of local footpaths the Group sought to encourage parishes to join the formal *Parish Paths Partnership* with County Councils. Membership of the scheme enhanced cooperation and information sharing when changes were proposed, diversions planned or put forward by owners and others.

With the growth in popularity of golf, the Group suggested suitable waymarking where rights of way cross existing courses, and advocated guidance for risky situations such as paths crossing fairways. The Society has developed a policy focusing on good environmental practice for golf courses

Changes to the path network

Paths are often affected by development and the Group's work frequently includes planning issues, so from time to time advice has been sought from the Society's Planning Team. ROWG officers regularly attend hearings where applications are presented for changes to the definitive maps. Several of these were exemplified in *Chiltern News* in September 1997. None became major issues but the list illustrates the extent of voluntary commitment. In addition to Group Chairman John Rowe's involvement, John Coombe (his successor), Janet Mitchell and Richard Boas of the ROWG were all participants at these hearings, each holding a particular brief and giving much personal attendance time.

A successful ROWG planning issue is described in *Chiltern News* by David Bounds of Area 8 in South Oxfordshire. Phillimore Estates were asked:

"… that a new path might be provided along their roadside field headland, linking together the ends of two existing paths." The request coincided with Oxfordshire County Council's intention to straighten the road at this point, bringing the inevitable increase in traffic speed … and risks to walkers.

"With the help of local County Councillor Alan Roberton, the modest cost of providing new access steps up the roadside bank and some extra hedge planting to screen the traffic, was included in the road scheme."(CN.144.)

Less efficacious was John Rowe's experience with the Berkhamsted bypass construction on the A41 dual carriageway. Here the completed work resulted in a potentially dangerous stepway down a steep bank to the road. Step construction was slipshod, there was no handrail, or fence at the bottom, to prevent a walker tripping or falling onto the (busy) roadway. After protracted negotiations with officials without result, John commented wryly:

"Unfortunately the Department of Transport accords low priority to the provision of road crossings for rights of way, especially in non-motorway standard trunk routes."

Further discussion did achieve a promise to review the situation and improve the quality of the steps leading down to the road.

Mapping the Territory - Bill Chester, cartographer par excellence.

From 1969 the Society began publishing its own footpath maps, giving prominence to Rights of Way. An initial attempt had been made by Christopher Wallis, with a map that gave greater width to the footpaths than to road features. However this did not succeed; the first maps were then drawn by Berenice Pedgeley. Her successor was Bill Chester, who took up the challenge, retiring in 1999 after 23 years. Of the 23 titles current in 2002, 22 were laminated – a recent popular improvement. The maps are produced to the same scale (1/25,000) as the Ordnance Survey Explorer print, but are smaller in overall size and easier to handle for short distance walkers.

Bill joined the Rights of Way Group early in the Society's life, and became Group Secretary for a time. Through walking in the Chilterns he came to appreciate the value of easily readable, handy-size maps. Thereafter he devoted his work for the Society to map cartography. His successor is Ted Swan, with major support from Nick Moon.

In 1993, Shire Publications, publishers of the maps until 2002, hosted a reception for Bill at the National Trust Information Centre, Ashridge, near Berkhamsted. The guests were taken on a guided walk around part of the Estate. This was followed by a cake cutting ceremony and appreciation attended by the Chairman of Herts County Council, the Mayor of Dacorum Borough, the MP for North-West Herts, Christopher Tatham, General Secretary of the Chiltern Society, and several other members.

At the Society's Annual General Meeting in 1999, Michael Rush paid tribute to Bill Chester, retiring after 23 years. By October 2002 around 250,000 maps had been sold since the first was produced; in recent years the Society has regularly received £1,000 annually in royalties.

Nick Moon – Rights of Way Group Research Officer

Nick Moon has been involved with the Chiltern Society since his final school days, in 1969. Nowadays he divides his time between Hamelin, where he teaches English to German adults from business, and the Chilterns, a place of leisure, relaxation and recreation that he has known since his school days. Peter Mould, third General Secretary of the Society, writing in *65-75 – The Chiltern Society's First Ten Years* places Nick in the context of the year 1975.

"This (the ROWG) was the first, and now the largest, of the (Society's) Groups with over 600 members. Support for the Group grew dramatically from 1967 to 1969 due to the Group's work on survey and clearance. The driving force behind this growth was Don Gresswell, Group Secretary for five years from 1968 to 1973. The Group's aims are to maintain public access by footpath and bridleway to the Chiltern countryside.

"(Their) remarkable record of achievement on footpaths was recognised by a Countryside Award in 1970. Many other people have contributed to the successes, not the least Jean Buchanan, Mary Wood and Brian Armstrong as successive Chairmen, Laurie Feacey and Tony Emery as Area Secretaries of long-standing and Nicholas Moon as the youngest local representative". (Vol 1. p15)

Nick's mother was Minutes Secretary to the Society's Council and her interest and enthusiasm encouraged him to take up membership of the organisation. He enjoyed walking, so the Rights of Way Group was the obvious choice, and this association has been maintained ever since. In his books he acknowledges the early influence of Don Gresswell upon his decision to become involved in conservation, the Chiltern Society and in particular, exploring the extensive footpath network which the ROWG was engaged in restoring.

Nick became passionately keen on all matters connected with the Chiltern countryside and, under Don's influence, found himself a volunteer footpath worker, assisting with clearance and extending the coverage of the Society's waymarking, helping to locate paths lost through years of neglect their use as rubbish dumps.

An Oxford university degree achieved, Nick, at Don Gresswell's suggestion, took on writing two books of country walks that Don had originally been asked to write. Subsequently Nick left England for Germany where he now works. In leisure time he improved his writing skills and style using them to provide detailed guides to the Chiltern countryside he loves and so much enjoys during his holidays at home in Stokenchurch. His publishers since 1989, the Book Castle of Dunstable, include nine of his volumes in their current list, three of these extending beyond the Chilterns across Oxfordshire including the Thames and Cherwell Valleys, and parts of the Cotswolds.

Nick has also advised and assisted Bill Chester for many years, taking a keen interest in the preparation of the Chiltern Society's own special footpath maps which Bill pioneered. Now that Bill has retired, Nick continues to assist, working with Ted Swan to produce new and updated versions of each map, and to include, where appropriate, the line of the Chiltern Way.

The Society's Millennium Project, to create a 200 kilometre circular walk through the Chilterns, was proposed to the ROWG by Rob Bethell. Nick was excited about this from the first and in full agreement with the proposal, planning it to visit as much of the best scenery as was possible. Nick writes:

"Rob's idea was to expand the route identified by Jimmy Parsons some years earlier, and this proved both practicable and acceptable to the ROWG. Later Rob master-minded the remedial work on the paths, the signposting and the waymarking. His contribution was equally vital with mine to the realisation of the project."

Nick's enthusiasm awakened, he immediately became engrossed in the design. John Coombe, Chairman of the Rights of Way Group commented that Nick did much of the surveying, plotting and setting the route while:

"… the rest of us followed Nick's direction, assisting Rob and getting on with the job of clearing and waymarking. John Rowe provided expert support where the route enters the North Chilterns round Luton and towards Lilley and Offley in Hertfordshire."

Nick wrote the *Chiltern Way guidebook* and, with the launching of two extensions, one north and one south, in October 2003, has produced the second and updated edition. The Chiltern Way is undoubtedly Nick's best achievement to date; he is one of the Chiltern Society's many enthusiastic working members, dedicated to conserving the Chiltern Hills and countryside in their unique beauty and as places for people to enjoy.

Freedom to Roam in the Countryside

The Department of the Environment, Transport and the Regions (predecessor of DEFRA) published its consultation paper *Access to the Open Countryside* in March 1998. The ROWG, the Chiltern Society's Bottom Wood Group, and the Society's Executive Council closely studied it. John Coombe wrote an explanatory note for *Chiltern News*:

"In preparing our response we had to recognise that many members have strong views for and against freedom. ... the Government is committed to ensuring greater access to open countryside and that the consultation paper was issued to seek views on how to achieve that objective rather than whether it was a desirable objective. Our response therefore concentrates upon issues such as resources, publicity (particularly mapping), comprising the rights of way network and the failure to deal adequately with woodlands." (CN.149.p26)

Later in the same year the Countryside Commission (re-organised in the late 1990s as the Countryside Agency), Government advisors on the countryside, published some thoughts on bringing the rights of way system into the 21st century (*Rights of Way in the 21st Century*). The Group's concern was that, despite the absence any direct relationship between this and the DETR's consultation, the Commission's ideas and proposals could become Government policy and be included in a related Bill.

There were three unsatisfactory proposals, which the Group strongly opposed. That:
- there should be a cut-off date after which claims to register a path after 20 years continuous use could not be made;
- that farmers and landowners should be able to secure quick decisions on diversions, and,
- that the resolution of decisions on map and path applications should be moved from the DETR to the County Councils.

The first proposal would, after a cut-off date, eliminate any possibility of disputed paths being registered. The Group noted three examples, where action would prove impossible if the proposals became law. These were at Siblets Wood (Chalfont St Peter); several long-established customary paths in South Oxfordshire; and at Chorleywood (Herts), where 19 unregistered paths had been identified.

> "The proposal is so offensive it is difficult to see why the Countryside Commission even suggested it. It offends a long-standing legal maxim 'once a highway, always a highway', and is retrospective."(CN.151)

John Coombe also noted that an owner or tenant must have been aware of the path's existence on obtaining title to the land, and therefore planned accordingly. He added "the proposal for disputes procedure ignored the advantage that the present system is seen to be fair".

Several critical issues were left out of the Commission's paper: the impact of new industrial and residential developments on rights of way; the trend towards fencing rural paths; road safety reference was 'thin'; there was no discussion on speed limits for narrow country roads, and no proposals to review the Inquiry system for resolving disputes.

The Countryside and Rights of Way Act, 2000 (CROW) enacted close variations of these proposals, and those for access to open countryside. The Countryside Commission (Agency) became responsible for the mapping essential to precise deliniation of access areas.

Foot and Mouth Disease

In 2001 the outbreak of Foot and Mouth disease brought immense frustration to the ROWG. All walks programmes were immediately suspended. By Easter some easement of the restriction was possible, but it proved a difficult year for all walkers, riders and cyclists in the countryside. From mid-July 2001, the Chilterns were declared free of the disease; on 14 January 2002 the control throughout Britain ended. However, in *Chiltern News* John Coombe reminded members:

> "This declaration is a relief but ... the official Code of Conduct still applies" (CN.163)

The Code provides a national frame of reference for all countryside users, warning them to avoid contact with animals, action needed in the event of contact, and on controlling dogs; staying on the designated paths, wearing clean gear and equipment, and ensuring that food and litter are not left in the countryside.

The contemporary Rights of Way Group (ROWG)

The activity and focus of today's Rights of Way Group is summarised by its Chairman thus:

- *Monitors* the condition of paths; reports problems to the Highway Authority (normally the County Council).
- *Maintains* paths; path representatives are encouraged to do minor clearance and waymarking. (For this we now use the Countryside Commission's colour formula.) Clearance and stile work is often referred to the Society's Mid-Week Conservation Volunteers (Path Maintenance Volunteers from 2002), many of whom are also involved in the ROWG.

- *Mulls* over strategic proposals to change rights of way rules and access. The Countryside and Rights of Way Act, 2000 (CROW), will involve much work.
- *Meditates* about proposals to change the path network: extinguishments, diversions, creations; negotiates and opposes at Inquiry (if appropriate).
- *Maps* the area to show paths more prominently than roads, to show open pubs and name them; Chiltern Society maps are prepared from actual surveys. New editions are offered in a laminated form.
- *Meets* to walk the Chilterns. Currently we have walks on Sunday mornings, mid-week mornings and a miscellany of other walks, eg the Ridgeway in even stages. We hold about 120 walks annually; a walked path is a good path. (Article for the History Project, May 2002)

Rights of Way Group and the Future

The Group engages in practical work to maintain the path network. Reviewing the changes during recent years, John Coombe says:

"County Councils tell us that rights of way budgets have been cut, yet public expectations are higher than ever. The Group, and the Mid-Week Conservation Volunteers can help with clearance of under/overgrowth, waymarking and stile work, but enforcement – blocked paths, failure to reinstate and roadside signs remain the Council's responsibility.

"There is much more consultation now. We have responded to a number of recent consultations from different bodies; now the Countryside and Rights of Way Act (CROW) is on the Statute Book there is to be further consultation before implementation, especially with regard to the designated areas and the related mapping.

"The Chilterns have only a modest amount of access land but we need to know the Rules. Rights of Way changes made by CROW need to be learned. County Councils have to produce improvement plans – we can help; landowners will have the right to submit diversion requests – previously County Councils had power to consider them, but no duty to do so, so more work here. Most far reaching is the cut-off date for adding existing paths to the definitive maps. This is to be achieved by collecting evidence from users and also available historical evidence.

"Over many years we have assisted local amenity groups to claim paths that, for one reason or another, have not been included in the definitive maps. Examples are Ibstone 23, Toddington 40, Goring 34, Swyncombe 36/37, Bledlow cum Saunderton 84. Perhaps the most important was Chenies 61 (in Mount Wood). A particularly contentious and protracted claim is at Siblet's Wood near Gerrards Cross. Sometimes we are able to negotiate a new path, preferably a right of way, but sometimes a permissive path is better than no result. In 1999 a permissive path overlooking the Chess near Latimer allowed for the elimination of half-a-mile of dangerous road walking in the Chess Valley. In 2002 the owners decided to dedicate the path formally, so it is now a right of way.

"Group effectiveness depends on membership strength in different Chiltern areas. For example, in recent years the recruitment of Tony Northwood as Area Secretary for Luton, South-Mid Bedfordshire (9a) plus Roger Partridge for Dacorum, has allowed John Rowe more time to cover South Bedfordshire/North Dacorum (9b), with beneficial results in each Area."

Celebrating the Millennium

In early 1999 Michael Rush and the Executive Council sought suggestions for a Millennium Project. In February, ROWG volunteered the concept of a 200 km circular walk round the Chilterns, to be called **The Chiltern Way**. Here was an idea; the story of how that idea grew is told by Rob Bethell elsewhere in this History. It was, and remains, an inspired achievement for the Society comparable with the Lacey Green Windmill (1986), the development of Bottom Wood and the Small Woodlands Project (1983 and continuing), the Chiltern Open Air Museum (1976), and the Ewelme Watercress Beds (1999). The way was extended in 2003.

Cycling in the Chilterns: the Cyclegroup

The group's beginning in 1997 was due largely to the enthusiasm of two members, Paul and Sue Thomas. They were joined by John Newman, and numbers increased steadily as its activities became more widely known. In 2000, Paul Thomas was able to announce that membership was 100.

By the following year, they had begun a cooperative route information service, and had established their own web site. Sights were set upon cooperation with the local authorities in establishing the Chiltern part of the national cyclists' network long promoted by *Sustainable Transport Ltd* (SUSTRANS). Paul reported that the Chilterns is surrounded by developing national routes, and local ways under consideration would connect with these major routes.

A regular programme of rides graded for both pace and distance has been developed gradually from the start; as the Group increased in size, so more leaders were found and more rides were added. The Society-wide membership survey brought over 200 expressions of interest for committee analysis and action. Because of the coincidence of interests, cyclists and horse riders are represented on the ROWG main committee, and the Cycle group is a sub-group of the Rights of Way Group. Following Paul and Sue Thomas' departure for East Anglia, John Newman, assisted by Alistair Phillips and other group members have organised the rides programme.

A 'Boots and Bikes' day, to focus attention on local cycle routes, was organised on18 Jun 2000 by Chiltern District Council. The intention was to present an occasion of interest to walkers and cyclists, exhibiting common purposes and interests. Well supported and backed by the Society's Mobile Shop, it was designed to coincide with the opening of three local routes named after former notable Chiltern persons. John Hampden, Parliamentarian and opponent of 17th century royal taxation, 'ship money'. Thomas Harding, yeoman of Aylesbury, charity founder and benefactor from Walton, and John Milton, poet and philosopher, who lived in Jordans near Seer Green.

In March 2002 Paul Thomas wrote in *Chiltern News* that he and Michael Hardy (Keeper of the Lacey Green Windmill) were working on a cycle route to be published in May 2000 in the *London Cyclist* as part of the London Cycling campaign.

"The route is a tour of Chiltern Mills and is due to be published … to coincide with National Mills week-end. … our ride on 12 May will be based on the route (of) about 80km in two 40km loops." Riders could choose shorter routes.

CHILTERN CONSERVATION VOLUNTEERS

From the first days of the Chiltern Society there was close cooperation between the Rights of Way Group and the Litter and Commons Group, the original conservation volunteers. The two shared the same founding member, Don Gresswell MBE. Where footpaths had become over-grown, or steps down steep places had decayed – whatever the task – frequently work parties were organised, often ad hoc, to cover a particular problem.

In 1983 Don Millar joined the Executive Council to represent the Litter and Commons Group. He was to remain an EC member for 18 years and, among many other contributions, experimentally carried out a membership drive in his area, Holmer Green, with remarkable success, thereby giving strength to Edward Newmark's plans. Throughout the years Don maintained a committed and interested connection with the wider Society concerns.

When Don Gresswell died in 1986, Don Millar assumed responsibility for the Chiltern Conservation Volunteers Bureau (CCVB, as it had become) work, remaining with it until his sudden death in 2002. He continued the close working relationship with the Rights of Way Group, organising footpath-clearing parties at weekends, and with the Mid-Week Conservation Volunteers. For a while there was a Sunday Group.

Don Millar also expanded the CCVB's work to include pond clearance, hedge-laying and trimming, and practical help in support of the Bottom Wood project, and at COAM. Much of this activity was carried out on a regular, and sometimes, an annual basis. In time some of the footpath work became the subject of formal contract, usually under the Parish Paths Partnership scheme; so effective were they that in 1996/97 the Conservation Volunteers brought more than £5,000 income to the Society.

In the 1990s the Group was formally divided into separate, smaller units working in an area or on a particular day each week. There were three primary groups: North, Central and South Chiltern Conservation Volunteers. A fourth, comprising mainly retired people and led by Ray Wainwright, and later Roy Crisp, Ron Horne and Eric Terry, was known as the Mid-Week Conservation Volunteers (Path Maintenance Volunteers from 2002).

Don Millar, supported by Group Secretary Christine Breden, remained overall organiser and co-ordinator. His was the Central Group; operational control in the north was placed with Julie Wilson who was Christine Breden's predecessor as Group Secretary. In the south, Beryl Hunt led the group (SCV) and planned the programmes.

Central Chilterns group

The December 1996 programme for the Central Conservation Volunteers, arranged by Don, contained a diverse range of activity. It included:

> "Working at the Chiltern Open Air Museum, Newland Park, Chalfont St Giles. Clearing old man's beard and tree guards from saplings and shrubs to enable them to grow in the spring of '97.
>
> "Work on Bledlow Cross keeping the area tidy and removing scrub encroaching onto the Cross. This was frequently done working with the HWBG Group members."

A one- to two-year project ("for us") was also forecast. The location was Rushymead Hospice, Amersham … a large, old house converted into a day centre for the elderly.

> "… the house used to look onto a man-made glade and pond area which has become overgrown with trees becoming too big. The pond has silted up and needs clearing and stinging nettles have taken over too much of the area. … The area is quite a haven for butterflies, and small birds of many types."

The work at Rushymead was guided by a watercolour painting of the glade in its heyday. Following Don's death, Christine Breden took over responsibility for the Central programme.

Mid-Week Volunteers group (Path Maintenance Volunteers from 2002)

The group decided, on establishment, to confine their activities to footpath clearance. (An earlier group, established in the Central/North Chilterns by Brian Armstrong, had followed a similar policy.) As news of their intention spread, their numbers increased. Membership was 40 strong when Don Millar took over as organiser, defining the tasks, towing the trailer and generally being the prime contact with the Society. During 1999/00 they made a significant contribution to path preparation and waymarking for the Chiltern Way, as Rob Bethell has mentioned in writing about the Society's Millennium Project.

The Society's annual reports and *Chiltern News* record some of the work carried out by the Group. In 1996/97 Group Leader Roy Crisp wrote:

> "This year has seen us involved in some major projects in the Amersham area, and Ley Hill Common. We have also been at work in Chalfont St Giles, Ashley Green and Beaconsfield. Our numbers have been usually around 15 (on each occasion) which means that we can really get something done".

South Chilterns group

During 1994, South Chilterns Conservation Volunteers under Beryl Hunt and Ken Smith's leadership had begun work on the next phase for restoring Highmoor Pond. This venture was a combined undertaking with the local community. A note in *Chiltern News* (September 1994) about the site and project, indicates the scope of the work.

"This acre-sized site is near Nettlebed, amidst farmland and beech woods, and a much used footpath passes close by. It is on common land, and was one of those 'lost' ponds until the local people decided to restore it. For many years, the site of this ancient pond has been used as a rubbish tip, but volunteers have spent more than 200 hours disposing of many cubic yards of rubbish that could be man-handled, and in tackling a large thicket of Japanese knotweed. To restore the site completely heavy plant must now be used to remove a large amount of remaining rubbish. Water drainage into the pond needs to be improved and the site graded to make a safe approach to the water."(CN.133.)

Don Millar's group assisted the South Chiltern Conservation Volunteers to get started and thereafter often joined them in large or interesting projects like Highmoor or at Ewelme Watercress Beds.

South Chilterns later worked on a joint venture involving the Nettlebed Commons Conservators. In the 1996/97 Chiltern Society's Annual Report, Beryl Hunt set out their year-long work programme.

"About half our work days have been spent on various parts of Nettlebed and District Commons. … The Commons Conservators have been awarded a Countryside Stewardship grant, with the aim of conserving this rapidly dwindling type of habitat.

"We work under the guidance of Rod d'Ayala, Assistant Warden at the BBONT Warburg Reserve, and Sally Rankin. … This sort of cooperative venture enables the volunteers to experience a wider range of conservation tasks and leaves the grant to be spent on specialist services that cannot be supplied by volunteers."

North Chilterns group

Julie Wilson, who had worked with Don Millar, initially led the Group. A report from the North Chilterns Volunteer Group during 1993/94 indicates similarly committed activity: the restoration of Breachwood Green Pond, a task in which the villagers joined, sharing the work. However in the longer term this Group ceased to be viable.

VOLUNTEER VALUE – AONBs COMPARED

The Chairman (Barry Scott) had been challenged during 1995 to say what was the cost effec-tiveness of volunteers and volunteering. He asked Group Chairmen to give him their estimate of the hours voluntarily worked during that year. He explained:

"We are increasingly asked for a quantitative statement rather than a qualitative description (of just) 'we believe in the Chilterns.'"

The results were a dramatic total of 21,348 hours committed by members during 1995. Repeating the exercise in 1996 produced almost another 2,000 hours more on the return, an increase of about 9%. Barry calculated that the monetary value of this activity at the "recommended rate" would be between £139,000 and £186,000. (This assumed an hourly rate between £5.9 and £7.9, lower, and therefore cheaper than some customary rates for comparable work in many other sectors of the economy at the time.)

Comparison between different AONBs is difficult. The nature of the environment, geographical structure, the terrain, river features, the number of footpaths, proximity to urban centres, levels of population, all make comparison difficult. Barry Scott thought the nearest AONB, although unique, "...but perhaps that most like the Chilterns in many ways is the Cotswolds..." about two and a half times the size. In 1994 its total of volunteer hours was 38,513. Allowing for the size difference, the widely spread, rural and sparsely populated areas, without urban pressures, the Chiltern figures compared favourably. The Cotswolds had a much larger budget, and 11 paid staff compared with the Chilterns' two. Both sets of work output numbers gave strong evidence of the value and public worth of voluntary work.

Also in 1995/96 Barry Scott and Michael Rush, then Vice-Chairman, visited three southern designated AONBs. Michael presented their findings in *Chiltern News* for September 1996. He reviewed the Cotswolds, East Hampshire, and the Sussex Downs, scheduling size, counties and districts, exceptional pressures on the AONB, population size and density, co-ordinating body (e.g. Chiltern Conference), paid staff, volunteers and annual income. His broad conclusion was that the Chilterns AONB was considerably under-resourced by comparison with the others, especially the Cotswolds. It suffered from a greater threat of urbanisation, had a greater density of population, and a lower level of budget income. Therefore the potential demands upon its resources were that much heavier. He raised the critical question that the Society faced:

"How should the Chiltern Society use its special position in this equation to promote the conservation and enhancement objectives?" (CN.141)

The question remained on the table; on becoming Chairman in 1997, it was one that Michael took up with some relish.

RIVERS, WETLANDS AND – WATER WATCHING

At their Annual General Meeting in November 1994 the Rivers and Waterlands Conservation Group (RWCG) adopted this new title; formerly it had been the Water Resources Group. This new name reflected more suitably the role and function that the Group now began to accept. For many years it had been chaired by Bernard Banfield who, supporting Vic Wotton, encouraged the Misbourne Rescue project. The Group Chaiman was now Don Brooks, an experienced water watcher from Dunstable in the north Chilterns area.

Vic Wotton had been the WRG Secretary for almost 14 years during which, with increasing success, the battle for the rescue of the Misbourne had been mounted and continued.

He now stood down from the administrative role; the Chiltern Society recognised his achievements and elected him one of its Vice Presidents. However, his efforts had demonstrated that conservation and water watching possess a broader perspective than the original Group title implied; factors that applied to the Misbourne might also be true of all the other rivers in the Chilterns.

During Vic's Misbourne rescue campaign, heightened public interest in water resources had been aroused following the privatisation of water services. The transition period from public to private ownership had been uneasy, coinciding with a time of reduced rainfall and drought conditions between 1987 and 1991. Rivers and reservoirs had lost water; water warnings were in force in some major cities; hosepipe bans were widely in operation and water supplies in less fortunate areas were delivered by tanker or through street stand-pipes.

Water Watchers

The Water Resources Group had originally established the role of Water Watcher and now recruited new members to them with considerable success; the newly titled Group continued the practice. Members who were keen to help observed and reported on river level and flow, boreholes were measured, corridor changes noted and reports sent to the Secretary at intervals. This is a task comparable with the careful work of footpath wardens from the ROWG, who report at intervals to their Area Secretary. In 1989/90 volunteers were appointed to watch over six Chiltern rivers and some of their tributaries.

Flow loss and alleviation in chalk streams

The campaign for the regeneration of the Misbourne had fostered two other significant developments. Where rivers appeared to be dying, there was an increasing concern for their revival. Secondly, there was a rising interest in the whole river corridor: flora, fauna, habitat, and linked landscape.

Vic's Rescue a River campaign led on to critical action for the Bulbourne and the Wye, and later systematic watches on the Gade, the Ver, and finally the Mimram. For all these rivers the problem of alleviation of low flows (ALFs) was raised with the privatised water companies and pressures exerted to secure reduced abstraction.

The increasing numbers of watchers, growing public awareness of water values, and RWCG's initiatives taken together, show that a momentum was achieved and an extended campaign begun, for the restoration and maintenance of Chiltern rivers and chalk streams. This provided the base upon which the future Chilterns Chalk Stream Project could be built.

The Northern Chilterns

Throughout 1995 and 1996, water watching developed significantly in the north Chilterns. Attention focussed upon the Mimram, the Hiz at Hitchin, and the Oughton with its wetland area. Ann Lohrey and her son recorded the efforts being made by several authorities, including Herts County and North Herts District Councils, to restore the Oughton Wetlands ecology.

David Hendon reported on Barton Springs in Bedfordshire in 1996 and 1997, and the difficulties encountered where stream flow had been previously diverted to serve the landowner's property. He said that the Barton site is a popular one: families' picnic, and children, dogs ("and even mountain bikes") paddle in the stream. This causes some disturbance to the ecological balance in the waters, disrupting the natural habitat.

River Corridors

The second development was a concern for the riverside corridors. In 1993, Ivor Brent, secretary of the Water Resources Group, initiated two practical study courses. They were designed to inform Group members about the diversity of life, flora and fauna, in what he termed a "healthy river corridor". This initiative engendered the idea of a survey and was taken up four years later.

The Chilterns Chalk Stream Project (CCSP)

In 1997 a project to improve the riverside corridors of the Misbourne and the Chess was initiated by Steve Rodrick, AONB Officer of the Chiltern Conference. A meeting, chaired by Sir John Johnson, Chiltern Society Vice-President and now Chairman of the newly titled shadow Chilterns Conservation Board, was arranged on site at Amersham. Representatives attended from local authorities, local associations and the Chiltern Society.

Reporting briefly upon the meeting *Chiltern News* noted a growing feature of the Society's work: the interaction between Groups and the partnership with the shadow CCB. The RWCG and other Groups would, necessarily, be involved in the river corridor project that developed into the Chilterns Chalk Stream Project (CCSP) across the AONB, managed by the Chilterns Conservation Board.

By the year 2000 two Society Groups were actively involved. Members contributed to CCSP practical workshops on the Rivers Chess and Wye, and the Hambledon Stream, organised by Sarah Bentley, the Chalk Streams Project Officer for the CCB. Group members assisted with guided riverside walks that became part of the Project. The activity as a whole served to reinforce existing collaborative links between the Society and the new Board.

John Norris had become Chairman of the (again renamed) Rivers and Wetlands Group, and has written that:

"The RWCG is represented on this Project"'s Steering Group. Close working with the CCSP is enabling the Group to diversify its interests. Water *quantity* remains a key issue and alleviation plans are in the pipeline for the Rivers Wye and Bulbourne, but the Group is becoming more involved with water *quality*, especially the restoration of riverine habitats that support unique flora and fauna associated with classic chalk streams." (letter, January 2003 to the Chiltern History project)

Chilterns-wide activity

The years 2000 and 2001 brought an increase in Water Watchers' work. Observations were extended to the Hamble and Ewelme Brooks in the South Chilterns; attention was given to the Hughenden Stream, and the Alderbourne – which Dr Arnold Baines called the "forgotten stream". Wainhill Spring and Cuttle Brook, below the scarp, and Cowhill Spring by Pitstone, were the subject of report. The last named had filled the moat at Moat Farm for the first time in many years. This undoubtedly delighted Bernard Banfield, founder member, in his 95th year, who had drawn attention to the Spring ten years previously and campaigned for its inclusion on the definitive map.

Ponds and still waters

At its November AGM in 1995 the RWCG had decided to review the still water sources. Nick Blakeney-Edwards, recently retired, offered to survey the Chiltern ponds shown on the OS Pathfinder maps. His report (1996/97) identified 932 ponds, many dry, some in need of rescue and many needing care. The majority (587) were on private land, and many that were adjacent to public footpaths were also privately owned. 177 of those on common land, or with "apparent" road access, were visited. The exercise concluded with 93 full survey reports.

Nick wrote:

"These show that many ponds were dry, some were closer to marsh than pond, some were foul and rank (but still harbouring life) and some were straight off a picture postcard. Ewelme was a classic example of the last category." (CN.144.p8/9)

Water in the South Chilterns

Action over water in the south was taken largely in the context of volunteer work programmes. The South Chilterns Volunteers (SCV) led by Beryl Hunt and Ken Smith took on a number of tasks that involved streams and rivers. At Goring-on-Thames an ancient millstream clogged with vegetation and a rotting tree trunk was cleared. Highmoor Pond near Nettlebed received attention over three years, clearing the rubbish and detritus including (it was said) the frame and chassis of a 1930s' bus dumped over 70 years before.

Lewknor watercress beds, no longer in commercial use, were weeded and cleared to enable the fast flowing stream to be better channelled. The Cotmore and Nuney Green ponds and the pond at Harpsden Court were cleared. Robert Watson, a Society and group member spent much time "working almost single-handed" to clear and resuscitate Hodmore Pond. Work was done at Ewelme as Nick Blakeney Edwards' survey had recorded.

The SCV took on other related tasks too: towpath maintenance around Thames-side seats at Goring-on-Thames and the immense and continuing task of restoring the Watercress Beds at Ewelme with the object of creating a nature reserve on a site. This had regional and, possibly, national environmental interest.

THE 30TH ANNIVERSARY PARTY – SWANS ON THE MISBOURNE –15 JULY 1995.

"Wonderful! Brilliant! Absolutely Marvellous!" These were the opening words of Cic Upcott's *Chiltern News* report of the celebrations. It was an occasion which blended the sounds of baroque music, with the enthusiasm of traditional jazz, rowing on the lake, crossing the weir to feed the swans (called Beethoven and Tchaikovsky) and cygnets, and cross back again over the walkway through the wetlands; it gave the opportunity to wear (and buy) one of the new Chiltern Society sweat shirts, and above all, to enjoy the wide variety of food: pastas, salads, bread and cheeses, followed by fruit pie with cream or custard. And all of this was preceded by, or accompanied with a selection of meats served (hotly) from three huge barbecues presided over by Derek Upcott and Russ Preston. There was more to follow after supper:

"At 9 o'clock we upped seats and removed to the natural amphitheatre beyond the ha-ha where tea and coffee were continuously being served by Marjorie Brooks and Di Millar in the summer house … A stage had been set up for our singers from Tring and we were splendidly entertained for another hour, with the intermission devoted to the grand raffle draw.

"So the dusk settled, the coloured lights on the stage and house began to glow and who will forget the horses prancing about on the skyline? It was idyllic, indeed a night to remember."

The event was held at the home of Michael Rush, Vice Chairman of the Society who, with his wife Linda and a small committee, planned and organised the occasion enjoyed by 250 members and friends. The report concludes:

"Many thanks to all the helpers, old and young who slaved in the heat putting up the small marquees, the tables, the chairs and barbeques, the lights and exhibitions, who cooked and served the food (a lot of work went into this particularly from Linda, who had the ideas, and shopped, and cooked a lot, and her team), the walk organiser, the car park attendants, the background boys (boys? Some were 80!), but above all to Michael Rush, the organiser par excellence."

A last pleasure was added when, as guests left in the growing darkness, they found their path to the car park traced by:

"a glowing line of lighted nightlights in white paper bags, half full of sand. I wonder if Linda knows how this final touch captivated many of us?"

NEW GOALS, NEW DEVELOPMENTS, NEW TARGETS

The nine years covering the chairmanships of Barry Scott and Michael Rush were those of immense change in the organisation and influence of the Society. Membership increased, involvement with statutory and shadow statutory bodies became greater; a specific marketing strategy brought a wider public awareness of the Society's work, and a diversity of activity began which carried the organisation forward to a record membership number. Most critically the Society engaged in a strategic review that resulted in a fundamental change to its constitution, creating a stronger basis for future expansion and growth.

These changes, and others with which they coincided reflected a rising national and international interest in the conservation of the environment. Popular feeling in Britain began to look to its better management and a distinct reduction in environmentally destructive human activities including the production of 'greenhouse gases'.

This popular feeling, whilst not directly connected with the Society's programmes, nevertheless raised public expectations and interest in environmental matters. Planning became pre-eminent, as did interest in leisure, amenity, conservation of resources, and problems of environmental pollution and distress.

Transition and change

Michael Rush became Chairman at the Annual General Meeting in October 1997. He succeeded Barry Scott and immediately after the election and close of business presided over an Open Forum. Introduced in 1983 by Charles Mills, the Forum had become a vital part of the AGM, during which members raised matters of their interest, generally without prior notice.

This Forum brought out a variety of members' interests some of which were to be followed vigorously during the next five years. The Wycombe Borough's plans for housing at Grange Farm, and the future of the Chinnor Cement works topped the list; both were to receive careful attention from Geoffrey Legge, Planning Co-ordinator. Don Brooks raised the matter of greater statutory powers for the national Environment Agency overseeing the privatised water industry. A straw poll revealed a substantial number in favour of a Society attempt to secure speed limits on all non-A and B class roads in the Chilterns.

Concluding the discussion, Michael Rush forecast greater and increasing responsibilities for the Executive Council. He also urged the need to make the Society more attractive to new members, to seek an enlarged membership, and to establish new projects. During the 12 months that followed, the pace of progress quickened as the EC began to respond to these challenges.

Changing pace - up to speed

Chairman Michael Rush's next Annual Report in 1998 detailed some of the changes being made by the Chiltern Society and he reviewed the various activities engaged in by the specialist Groups during his first year of office.

He commended the ROWG for its continuing campaign to reduce the number of stiles inhibiting a walker's progress; he wished them success in securing reductions in road walking, and he commended the Group's response to the *Freedom to Roam* consultation paper. Michael and his wife Linda had joined the first cycle run organised by the newly established Cyclegroup and they had much enjoyed the experience.

He expressed pleasure that Christopher Wallis has been able to take over the Chair of the Historic Works and Buildings Group. He noted the successful outcome of the River Misbourne project, that John Norris had succeeded Don Brooks, and Jean de Selincourt had been elected Secretary of the Rivers and Wetlands Conservation Group. Michael said how excellent had been the work of the Conservation Volunteers under Don Millar, and praised the South Chilterns Volunteers' pond restoration activities at Bix where they had linked with the village Millennium celebrations.

Working in partnership with the Chiltern Conference (shadow CCB) was, for him, an important strategy. 52 million tourist visits had been recorded in a survey of 16 sites in the Chilterns in one year; the Area needed special protection and care:

"… as one of the independent members of the Chiltern Conference, we are particularly well placed to lobby our MPs on this issue."

The Society's Planning Group had been very active throughout the year. Under Geoffrey Legge's leadership they were at the "leading edge of some of our most important work".

Finally, Michael Rush listed a number of matters about which he was especially excited and encouraged. Response to the Penn Wood appeal had been excellent enabling the Woodland Trust to complete its purchase. He welcomed Richard Burton as the new Press Relations Officer. The Chilterns Buildings Design Guide lines were being worked out and the Society was making a significant contribution to their formulation.

The Chairman also reported changes affecting the Executive Council. Early in 1998 the Executive Council procedures had been reviewed, and members were asked to consider whether the Society needed professional help with its development, role and function. A Strengths, Weaknesses, Opportunities and Threats (SWOT) exercise had been used to focus thinking upon forward planning. The initial outcome was that a Marketing Working Party had been set up and briefed to propose a strategy for the more effective public presentation of the Society.

Finally, the Chairman paid tribute to Cic Upcott and the *Chiltern News* Editorial Team for the upgrade of the magazine and its first publication in colour. *Chiltern News* was, he thought, the primary means of communicating with the Society's growing membership. The quality of the production was very high.

At the end of the meeting Philip Hanscombe, a member who had been responsible for PR in ICI Paints, approached Michael Rush and congratulated him on his speech. He asked

Michael if he himself had been in PR!

Philip offered to help in any way he could and Michael never one to miss an opportunity to get a real expert on board, appointed Philip as Society PRO, which he has been ever since, very much at one with the Chairman's wish for good publicity.

A New Image: the Chiltern Society Logo

During 1999, a long discussed matter was finally resolved with the help of Countryside Commission's consultants. A new logo evocative of the Chiltern Hills replaced the pollarded beech tree that, in silhouette, had been the Society's symbol from its earliest years. The new image fitted well with the endeavour to improve the Society's public image.

Debates about the logo had occurred over several years; the decision taken, the presentation of the fair copy was made by John Craven from BBC TV Country File programme, a resident of the Chilterns. Fittingly the event took place at Lacey Green Windmill, the first of the Society's major project achievementson the Sheath to Loaf Village Day. Michael Rush, in reporting this to the AGM, paid tribute to Michael Hardy, whose organisation of the event made it a very special occasion.

New developments, new schemes

Michael Rush, when Vice Chairman, had already been one of the Society's representatives to the Chiltern Conference. Now, as Chairman he aimed to strengthen the relationship where it seemed useful and appropriate.

The Buildings Design Awards competition was first among the new developments promoted in collaboration with the Conference. Initially co-ordinated by Tad Effendowicz, and thereafter by Jenny Habib, the entries were judged by an expert panel, chaired by Sir John Johnson, and the Awards presented at a ceremony in May.

The purpose of the Scheme was to raise awareness of good building design in the Chilterns. The assessors considered appearance, imaginative and innovative design, use of materials, relationship to neighbouring buildings and the environment, energy efficiency, and the final landscaping. Buildings entered must have been completed within the previous three years. The 1998 Award went to Ballinger Village Hall, near Great Missenden.

In the 2001 competition, the Awards attracted 28 entries. The winner was Hunts Green Barn, Henley, with four others in the Highly Commended category, and a further five receiving Special Letters of Commendation. The prizes were presented at Chesham Town Hall by Chiltern Society member, Lucinda Lambton, the well-known TV presenter and expert on traditional buildings.

The acquisition of **Ewelme Watercress Beds** was second on the new developments list during 1999. The Chairman looked forward to the completion of this ambitious venture, part of the South Chilterns Volunteers' work. A campaign was launched by the Society with the patronage of Jeremy Irons to raise funds for the Beds' purchase, restoration and management. Beryl Hunt, whose crusade this was, had described it to Harry Cook (Chairman 1988/93)) as the South Oxfordshire 'Windmill', because of the extent of the commitment, recalling Lacey Green's 20 year span.

Like the Building Design Award, the venture was a cooperative effort involving several organisations: the Friends of Ewelme, the Local Heritage Initiative, the Heritage Lottery Fund, and the Chiltern Society. A short, evocative book, *The Story of Ewelme Watercress* by John Legh, was published by the Friends in support of the campaign.

The previous year's challenge, for **action over of speed limits on country roads**, had been picked up by a small working group consisting of Derek Upcott (Vice Chairman), Edward Newmark and Guy Patterson. They were to analyse the problem and propose solutions that might be adopted as Society policy.

Two other developments received the Chairman's mention in his first year's report. Dave Howarth was asked to review the **Local Members' group structure**, building on the S & I Groups begun by Harry Cook and encouraged during Barry Scott's period of office. Last, a **Schools Liaison Team** was appointed to help raise awareness of environmental issues among children and teachers.

STRATEGY FOR THE 21ST CENTURY – NEW HORIZONS

To build upon the progress of the Chiltern Society during the period up to 1999, Michael Rush invited Robin Rowland, a long-time member and supporter, to review its activities and future opportunities. Robin had just retired from a distinguished business career that involved contact with national and international voluntary organisations. Chiltern Society membership was increasing; it seemed the right moment for a strategic review and to consider its future.

Robin brought an energetic, enthusiastic and informed approach to the task. On receiving an initial report the Executive Council decided to set up a Strategic Planning Team (SPT) to prepare specific proposals for the Society for the next five to ten years. Robin was invited to become the second Vice Chairman of the Society and to chair the Team.

A personal challenge

He has written an account in which he describes clearly the process of his first study and the Team's subsequent Report. The writing expresses his great feeling for the work:

"It was the summer of 1999 when John Taylor, the Society's Treasurer, approached me and suggested that the Chairman would be interested in meeting with us. It was not long before the Rush subtle persuasive magic started to work. He suggested correctly that I must have had to review many organisations in my previous job. He then showed his vision by suggesting that just when both inside and outside the Chiltern Society people felt that the Society was doing very well was the time to carry out a low key study of how the Society should adapt itself for the future.

"I had been lucky enough to be able to choose to retire early in 1998 from a job that I was still thoroughly enjoying, being paid to travel the world for nearly 20 years looking at a range of small and large organisations in over 50 countries. I had also been my company's Worldwide Community Relations Director and this had brought me into contact with some inspirational social entrepreneurial community projects and non-profit organisations. My rather unstructured plan was for a second career using my experience and knowledge to help a range of non-profit organisations both internationally and in the UK."

For Robin this meant that he would now have a way of contributing to the area that he and his wife had lived in and loved since 1982 but which, because of his absences overseas, had been unexplored. He had been a 'sleeping member' of local organisations including the Chiltern Society, although in touch with the latter through the "excellent *Chiltern News*" that often travelled with him on his worldwide journeys.

Next he was invited to attend an Executive Council to discuss an outline brief for the study. Robin's account continues:

"Within two short weeks of that, Tony Balfour, the General Secretary was on the doorstep asking me to accept nomination to the Executive Council at the forthcoming October AGM. The proposed study was announced and at its subsequent meeting the EC agreed the terms of reference. My life was about to change!"

Options for the Future: the way forward
The study was titled *The Way Forward – Options for the Future*. The Report would be based on interviews inside and outside the Society. In addition, Robin undertook to review earlier Executive Council papers, read the short histories, and other useful background material. Members of the EC were invited to make verbal or written contributions, and people to whom he spoke were asked to recommend others whom he should see. Obvious names came up many times such as the Countryside Agency, and Steve Rodrick, the AONB Officer. Less prominent ones ("at least to me") were the Herts Countryside Management Services at Hitchin, and the Countryside Landowners Association at Newbury.

"Over a period of five months I conducted some 50 interviews. Travelling from Goring-on-Thames to Hitchin, Ibstone to Lacey Green was a great way for me to get to know the lovely area that is the Chilterns. But what really impressed me was the enormous commitment and professionalism of so many people inside the Society and the equally enormous goodwill towards and respect for the Society from others. I recall a wonderfully informative discussion with Edward Newmark, Membership Secretary at his home, followed by a equally useful one in Oxford with Martin Spray, Director of the Bucks, Berks, and Oxfordshire Wildlife Trust (BBOWT).

"There was clearly tremendous scope for working with others. It was a wonderful education for me, visiting and talking with so many enthusiastic carers for the Chilterns, but several things stood out from the feedback I was receiving and so, in July 2000, I presented my Report to the Executive Council. It was titled: *The Chiltern Society in the Year 2000*."

Robin's Report identified six key issues in addition to other recommendations:

- Form a Group to prepare a five-year Strategic Plan and Vision and develop from that a two-year Business Plan.
- Convert the Society into a Company Limited by Guarantee in line with the practice of many medium to large voluntary organisations. (Its status at the time was that of an unincorporated association of unlimited liability on the part of all members.)
- Organise and carry out a Membership Survey and from this construct a new, improved database to give a better understanding of members' interests, skills, and capacities.
- Carry forward and enhance the Membership campaign.
- Investigate the prospect of a major schools and adult Chilterns Environmental Education Initiative.
- Provide more secretarial support for Christine Preston, the Society's Administrator.

Executive Council's response

The EC responded quickly; it discussed and agreed the recommendations. A strong Strategic Planning Team, representative of a wide range of interests, was appointed and Robin Rowland was invited to be its Chairman. He records his own re-action

"To be honest I was not too reluctant because the team was such a strong one with such a range of interests and experience. By now I could see what a worthwhile role the Society had played and would play in the future as the organisation totally dedicated to caring for the whole of the Chilterns. It was independent, thriving, growing in its influence (membership had increased by another 1000 on the previous 12 months.) and it was delivering really worthwhile projects such as creating the Chiltern Way and saving the Ewelme Watercress Beds."

His team members were: Betty Hardy (Historic Works and Buildings), David Howarth (Members' Group Planning), Mark Januszewski (Planning Team Secretary), Geoffrey Larminie (Geological and Environmental Adviser), Geoffrey Legge (Planning Co-ordinator), Edward Newmark (Membership Secretary), John Norris (Rivers and Wetlands Conservation), Paul Thomas (Cycling group), and Cic Upcott (Editor, *Chiltern News*). The Group was assisted and advised by Professor John McGee from Warwick University, a Society member, and clerked by Helen Nolan.

Small sub-groups were set up to consider particular Society features. Dave Howarth led one to prepare the way for the Membership Survey and Database to be implemented in the spring of 2001. Many detailed supplementary position papers were produced: in particular, by Geoffrey Larminie on *Farming*, John Norris on *Water Resources*, and Michael Hardy on the *Historic Heritage*.

Between the first meeting on 3 August 2000, and the publication of the final Report, the Team, all volunteers, put in an estimated 900 hours of time. Robin comments:

"This reflected to me the commitment that is so evident in so many people of diverse interests in the Society, who passionately care for the Chilterns."

Caring for the Future of the Chilterns by planning for the 21st Century

Perhaps the most important outputs were the two visions:

Our Vision for the Chilterns in the 21st Century, and

Our Vision for the Society for the next Ten Years

These were published on the Society's web site, in *Chiltern News*, and in the Annual Report for 2000/01. The national Chief Executive of the Civic Trust complimented the Society on its efforts, and described them as "examples for all others to follow."

The Review recommendations

- Continue to uniquely focus on the Chilterns.
- Continue strong commitment to conservation of the natural environment as well as its historic sites and buildings.
- Maintain a strong, co-ordinated approach to planning proposals.
- Increase the Society's focus on farming issues in the Chilterns.
- Continue to implement projects on a regular basis.
- Remain an organisation run by, and largely dependent on volunteers.
- Develop the work of the Chiltern Conservation Volunteers.
- Raise awareness and understanding of the character and history of the Chilterns through schools, by all ages, to encourage them to enjoy and care for its natural environment and beauty.
- Remain non-political and independent.
- Take advantage of modern technology.
- Communicate regularly between Groups and with members.
- Adapt Executive Council and other meetings to meet the needs of the organisation.
- Reach the membership target of 12,000 by the end of 2005.
- Communicate regularly and clearly with the outside world.
- Work closely with other organisations that care about the Chilterns.

There were 80 detailed recommendations in the Report, supporting the principles set out above. Many affirmed what was already happening. However, the main theme was the need to attract more volunteers to achieve the objectives the Society was setting itself. The Chiltern Society was found to be as relevant and essential as it was when founded. The Membership Survey later in 2001 emphatically confirmed this and the active interest of many members in being involved in caring about the area where they live.

In January 2001 the Executive Council approved the Report, agreeing both the Visions and the recommendations. These have become the policies and strategies informing the Society's progress into the 21st Century.

Strengthening the foundations - a company limited by guarantee

An early action generated was the alteration of the Society's structural base. For more than 30 years it was an unincorporated voluntary organisation: all its members were potentially liable for all the Society's debts. This formula is sufficient and satisfactory for small community groups, but with the ever-widening range of activities, many physical in nature, steps had to be taken to protect the membership, in particular the Executive Council members.

During the decade from 1992 the Society had become both larger and more complex in its activities and aspirations. A different structure was needed: rules that limited members' liability had become essential. The Strategic Review offered an opportunity to consider this and to amend the Society's constitution to fit its changing status.

Ray Challinor, a member with many years of commercial experience, offered to help the process forward once the recommendations had the Executive Council's approval. The change proved relatively easy, as Ray described:

"The starting point was the Annual General Meeting for 2000 when members agreed in principle that we should proceed as proposed. The actual process was quite straightforward and was accomplished within the timetable agreed by the Executive Council.

"The first task was to form a small Working Party to review the existing Constitution, with a view to retaining as much as possible but having regard to the requirements of the Companies Act. We wanted the change to be as seamless as possible, and saw no need to re-invent the wheel as far as our various objectives were concerned. In effect, the old Constitution had to be revised and produced in the form of a Memorandum and Articles of Association (M&A) for a Company Limited by Guarantee. The change meant that members would undertake to provide a maximum of £1 each if called upon in the event of the Company becoming insolvent.

"The opportunity was taken also to fine tune the existing Objects as set out in the Constitution. Remarkably little was changed which is a tribute to the foresight of those founding the Society in 1965.

"Once the M&A had been agreed by the Executive Council the next step was to form and register a new company. This created a separate and distinct legal entity. That took only a few days.

"Next we had to form a new Charity using the M&A as our Constitution because it was not possible in law to convert the then existing charity (No.247000) to a limited company."

The Trustees were required to sign up to the new charity in preparation for a formal application to the Charity Commissioners; this would deal also with the transfer of assets and liabilities from the old to the new charity (No.1085163).

The agreement for the transfer was signed by Michael Rush, Chairman of the Chiltern Society, and Ray Challinor, General Secretary, and witnessed by Rowena Challinor on behalf of the membership. Ray's personal account of the process continues:

"In due course we received consent (from the Charity Commission) and all that then remained was for the Society's membership to formally ratify the proposal, and this was done at a Special General Meeting held on 18 May 2001."

The Society's name remains unchanged, but it is required to describe itself on its literature and letters as *a company limited by guarantee*. The change in status has resulted in the virtual elimination of members' liabilities, and for all practical purposes the same applies to the Trustees, apart from their financial and supervisory liabilities as Trustees.

Ray's account of the procedures ends by recording:

"The formal documentation giving effect to the decision was completed on 30th June with the new charity operating from July 1, 2001."

A new chapter of the Society's history had been started.

NEW ACHIEVEMENTS, NEW SUCCESS - IN THE 21ST CENTURY

The Chiltern Way – Project for the Millennium, written by Rob Bethell

Early in 1999 the Society gave thought to possible ways by which it could celebrate the Millennium. A number of proposals were considered but nothing was forthcoming that was significantly different from the host of projects under consideration by just about every society and parish in the country. That is until Michael Rush, Society Chairman, asked the Rights of Way Group Committee to come up with ideas. There was only one suggestion, for a long distance circular walk round the Chilterns. This was exactly the sort of Millennium Project needed because it encompassed the Society's ideals, was uniquely different from most other projects and one that was of potential lasting benefit for the Chiltern area.

The Project caught the imagination of the Society and many members became involved with publicity, fund raising and producing computerised maps of the route. 15,000 leaflets describing the Project were designed and widely distributed. One of the most satisfying features was the fantastic response from the rank and file Society members. It had been proposed that members who contributed £25 or more to the Project would become Founder Members of the Chiltern Way and would receive a free copy of the guidebook, as well as an invitation to the launch event.

It was estimated that a budget of £14,500 might be required to cover costs of materials, waymarking and transport. Response was beyond all expectations and the total sum raised from this and other donations from local authorities, parishes, business, and the 'Millennium Festival Awards For All', far exceeded the final expenditure.

Jimmy Parsons, a Society member, had devised a 100km circular route about 10 years previously, called The Chiltern Hundred. The name was attractive but the route wasn't quite what was wanted. Fortunately ROWG Research Officer, Nick Moon, offered to choose the route and write the guidebook – two major problems solved. In hindsight, perhaps the most significant factor for success was this contribution. At the time most of us accepted the route without too much thought and got on with the job of getting it cleared out and waymarked. However, since then there have been many references to the high scenic quality of the route and the excellence of the guidebook.

The route was chosen to cover as much of the Chilterns as possible including the area north of Luton. It would use existing rights of way but not exclude permissive paths where these were of benefit; it would have good views and, to a slight degree, utilise underused paths. The distance would be just over 200km and the route would pass through four counties, 10 districts, and 60 parishes. The designation The Chiltern Way was proposed and adopted by the Executive Council.

The route was split into sections and surveyed by members of the ROWG; Area Secretaries and Mid-Week Conservation Volunteers under Don Millar were persuaded to carry out clearance and maintenance work. Necessary waymarking was done by ROWG linked with the Volunteers. The practical side of the Project was co-ordinated by Rob Bethell.

Over 1,500 waymark discs were used, and 550 specially designed finger pointers were installed. In woods where discs could not be used, white arrows and CW were painted on trees where it was necessary to define the route. Most of the work was carried out between November 1999 and June 2000

Rob's wife, Ann made an important contribution to this phase of the work. She drove Rob from point to location point, enabling him to assess the route and later to waymark some sections. Ann also became very skilled in the practice of waymarking and the installation of finger pointers. Her contribution and his were recognised by a special Award made by Michael Rush on behalf of the Chiltern Society. The work of the many volunteers was acknowledged by calling them Founder Helpers.

The necessary procedures were taken to get the Chiltern Way marked as a long distance path on future copies of the Ordnance Survey and Chiltern Society maps. Details were sent also to the Long Distance Walkers' Association for incorporation into their handbook. It is of interest that the Chiltern Way of 215km is number 40 for distance. When the hilly nature of the terrain is also taken into account the route should not be considered as an insignificant ramble.

Between May and August 2000 12 walks were organised to allow members to do sections of the Chiltern Way. These were very popular and eventually 15 members completed the full round and, together with those who had already completed the walk when carrying out survey work, were all nominated Founder Walkers. With the tremendous support from Society members the whole Project was completed well within the time schedule and also well under budget.

The official launch occurred at Coleshill, near Amersham, on Sunday 22 October 2000. Two groups of walkers converged on All Saints church at midday. They were met at the Millennium lychgate by Olympic gold medallist Chris Brasher, who had himself just walked in from Penn, Michael Rush the Society's Chairman, and Sir John Johnson, President of the Long Distance Walkers' Association and a Vice President of the Society.

A reception for nearly 200 guests, including Founder Helpers and Walkers, was held in the village hall nearby. Special guests included Cheryl Gillan, MP for Chesham and Amersham and Michael Meacher MP, Minister of State for the Environment. During the speeches, the Minister was very supportive of the Society's work in maintaining the amenity value of the Chilterns, and Chris Brasher expressed his amazement at the amount of work that had been done to establish the Chiltern Way in such a short period of time. The Society had a right to be justly proud of its achievement.

Writing about the project a year later Rob Bethell added:

"We are aware that there are a few places where the original route is less than perfect and there is still a chance that the odd improvement might be possible. For instance, we are trying to get officialdom to accept responsibility for lighting the dark tunnel under the M40 motorway at Flackwell Heath. However, a much-improved crossing of the Luton to Bedford railway now exists. A newly constructed pedestrian bridge is in place about 80 metres beyond the original crossing point."

"So many Millennium Projects are a one-year wonder and are then forgotten. The Chiltern Way has been established as a popular long distance walk. I think we can be proud of our achievement and it is our intention to maintain the high standard that we set ourselves initially. Perhaps just as important for those directly involved with the Project, it has been good fun."

Extension in 2003: postscript by Rob Bethell

When the Chiltern Way was originally devised its extent was limited by what could be achieved in October 2000. Nick Moon proposed extensions to the north and south of the old route. These were walked, commented upon, alternatives proposed and two interesting routes finalised in early 2003. The two extensions cover some impressive and, in parts, rarely visited Chiltern scenery and should prove a new challenge to those walkers who thought they had completed the Chiltern Way.

The Northern Extension of 27 miles leaves the old route at Sharpenhoe Clappers, goes via Barton and Pegsdon Hills, Great Offley, Preston and Whitwell and rejoins at Peter's Green, bypassing 15 miles of the original Way. The Southern Extension runs from close by

Maidensgrove to near Ewelme via Greys Court, Mapledurham, Goring and Woodcote, adding 31 miles and bypassing five. It is the intention to maintain both the original route and the extensions. Nick Moon has written an extended and updated guidebook that will be published to coincide with the official opening of the extensions on 19 October. Waymarking is underway by Ann and Rob Bethell. The greater Chiltern Way created by these extensions now traverses 261 km (163 miles) and fully represents the AONB countryside.

Ewelme Watercress Beds – Heritage Rescue, a remarkable achievement

Begun by Beryl Hunt several years before, but carried forward into the momentum of new activity was a massive work project, which involved South Chilterns Conservation Volunteers constantly, and CCV with Don Millar from time to time, aiming to rescue and restore the Watercress Beds at Ewelme. These beds are a particular, special conservation case. Following a public appeal the Beds were purchased by the Society in order to achieve full restoration and retain an example of an indigenous Chilterns industry.

Their likely future is as a sanctuary for wild life, flora and fauna. In 1994 their continuance was in doubt with the prospect of a land sale for development, thus permanently destroying a feature of Ewelme that was probably created following land purchase by George Smith of South Weston, in 1886. (John Legh. *The Story of Ewelme Watercress*. 1999).

Watercress is an ancient garnish and an ingredient of salad in more recent times. Wherever chalk streams rise and flow smoothly, man has cultivated watercress. In the 1880s, 1890s and into the early 20th century the beds at Ewelme daily supplied Birmingham, the Midlands and many other markets with fresh watercress, sent by the expanding branch railway system.

A meeting in the autumn of 1996 at the Village Hall received a progress report and heard a statement of aims. These were:

"to purchase the 6.5 acre site with the help of money from the Heritage Lottery Fund, and to manage it for its industrial archaeological, historic, wildlife and landscape value."

The meeting marked a huge step forward in a well-established local campaign, although almost three years elapsed before purchase became possible. Contributing speakers included the Chairman of South Oxfordshire District Council, the Oxford County Archaeologist, a Conservation Officer from the Environment Agency, and representatives from the Chiltern Society. The occasion was well and enthusiastically supported; the Project Committee announced its intention to investigate financial help from the Countryside Stewardship Scheme, once ownership had been achieved.

In 1999 a dramatic reduction in the asking price from £195,000 to £100,000 made feasible a second application to the Heritage Lottery Fund. At this point Hugh Hunt became involved. Since then, with the exception of the period of the actual fund-raising and legal work

(September 1999 - November 2000) both Beryl and Hugh Hunt have worked on the Project what would be normal full-time hours, and often longer.

In September 1999, after much preparation, an appeal for £125,000 was launched by Jeremy Irons to enable the purchase of the Beds and carry out necessary repairs. In less than six months £145,000 was raised and by November 2000 the purchase was completed. Work restarted immediately. A Management Committee was set up with representatives from the Parish Council, the Ewelme Society and the Friends, together with two specialist advisers and representatives from the Chiltern Society in whom the property is vested. By early 2002, Hugh Hunt, Chairman of the Management Committee, was able to report in *Chiltern News* that work had begun on the sluices, replacing the concrete bund (walkway) and that preparations for the Volunteer Centre were being made.

The Ewelme Project was, and remains, one of the great ventures for the Chiltern Society. It ranks with Lacey Green Windmill completed in 1986, and the Small Woodlands Project launched in 1983. The successful rescue is an immense tribute to the persistence of Beryl and Hugh Hunt, Society members and leaders of the South Chilterns Conservation Volunteers. They have been fully supported by Desmond and Avril Dix, water watchers, Society members, and leading members of the Friends of Ewelme of whom Desmond is Chairman.

PROMOTING AND RECORDING THE CHILTERN SOCIETY

PhotoGroup - bringing the Society into focus

The PhotoGroup was founded in 1991, following an initiative by John Wellsman who was also involved with the Historic Works and Buildings Group as Conservation Watchers' co-ordinator. At their first meeting John was elected Chairman and later Guy Patterson became Secretary, and Group representative on the Executive Council.

The Aims, defined at a further meeting, were threefold:

- to maintain a pictorial library,
- to record the Chiltern scene,
- to hold exhibitions.

The last of these was the starting point for the activity of the new Group. The first is now being followed with vigour, as is the central aim.

Initially members were pleasantly surprised to find that the Society had a small library of some 200 slides, taken in the 60s by persons unknown. Each was numbered sequentially, and it was clear that some were missing. However, as news of the Group's objectives got around the missing slides began to trickle back from forgetful borrowers.

In the following year (1992) the Group received 500 slides from the late Fred Mitchell's collection, and 200 from John Morgan. Most of these originated from the 60s. A few had deteriorated, but many were first-rate pictures with more or less adequate annotation. All were placed on a computer database and a printed catalogue was produced. Membership had grown meantime, from the eight attendees at the Inaugural meeting to a substantial 67 at the 1992 AGM. Guy Patterson, Group Secretary wrote in his recent report, that in 1995:

"The Library had grown to 1,206 slides, with 90 of these taken before 1960, thus the historic basis of the Library was substantial. This year we had received an unusual collection of photographic material from Frank Ghyssens. There were about 200 slides, six 8mm cine films, and a Bolex projector which, after slight adjustment was found to be in working order. Frank was a tireless cyclist and photographer with a keen interest in British crafts and customs.

"He travelled all over the UK but lived in the Chilterns. We show one or other of his films every year at our AGM, using his donated Bolex projector. We also received 120 slides taken by the late Don Gresswell, early activist of the Chiltern Society and Vice President until his death in 1986. In addition, a large collection came from the late Maurice Wooller ARPS. These are flower slides that include 115 species found in the Chilterns. CD roms appeared on the market at this time and offered a new method of storage and distribution for Library pictures."

Full representation on the Executive Council came in 1994 and with it, increased funding. This made possible the mounting of the Group's first exhibition at Chiltern Open Air Museum (COAM) in Newland Park. 50 prints were shown, and judged by James Moir, COAM's Director; four prizes were awarded.

During the following year the Group undertook to produce 10,000 Christmas cards. Five pictures were selected and printing was comparatively easy. Packaging, distribution and sales were less so, and it was found that the Society's profit was small. The enterprise was not repeated on this basis.

From early in 1996 the Group began to enlarge its activities. A new style, A5, eight page newsletter was produced. This offered a regular article of photographic interest; typical was Don Brook's article on X-ray photography in Issue No 4. Useful studies of Dunstable and Hitchin by Don, and Lane End by Simon Griffin, were added to the Library. Guy Patterson continued his report:

"Don Brooks had many a struggle photographing the westward flowing Chiltern chalk streams, with the Rivers and Wetlands Conservation Group. These streams often run in ravines cut deep into the limestone, with banks covered thickly with scrub vegetation. He reports that on one occasion while descending a very steep bank in order to get a view of the spring head he found himself in free fall over the last five feet; he finished up standing in two feet of water thick with watercress and rushes."

By the AGM in 1996, membership of the PhotoGroup had risen to 91, the first Puzzle Picture, the sundial on Watlington Town Hall, appeared in the June edition of *Chiltern News*, and the Group adopted a less formal title: PhotoGroup. Activity was greatly stimulated when, in 1997, the Group received a generous donation of £1,000 from Margaret Mitchell for the purpose of copying her husband's collection of 500 slides that the Library had gained in 1992. Work on this larger task was begun in 2000 and the completed copy slides were deposited at the newly opened administrative Office in White Hill Centre, Chesham.

In 1996 Barry Scott, the Chiltern Society Chairman, had written to all specialist Group leaders asking them to assess the number of man-hours spent on voluntary work in 1995. PhotoGroup proudly recorded 272.

From 1998 onwards the Group's exhibition practice changed. In that year, COAM could no longer accommodate the annual display. A small exhibition was organised at Westbrook Hay School, near Hemel Hempstead. Then for the next year Watford Museum, housed in the former Benskin's Brewery, was used, and this has continued. Prizes were awarded on the basis of visitor acclaim; a smaller exhibition was held at Uxbridge Library. In 2001, a large show was mounted in the foyer of Luton Library as well as the annual one at Watford.

Other recent activities include a photographing exploration of the Chiltern villages planned by various members of the PhotoGroup. The first one was at Hambleden and led by Arthur and Doreen Petty. Guy Patterson mentions that:

"Hambleden is a picturesque village with a consistent brick and flint style to the houses; many pictures were taken which perhaps accounts for the slight bias towards Hambleden shown in the autumn exhibition of 2000"

The recent activity of the Group reflects its development and strength of purpose in carrying forward its three primary aims. During 2001, members visited the Chinnor steam railway, studying the problems of photographing railway stock. Later in the year they went to Ewelme to photograph members at work on the newly acquired watercress beds. The church and almshouses there also attracted attention. For the Society Garden Party at Bledlow Manor a 15-picture quiz was set up. The two large exhibitions at Luton Library and Watford Museum were staged. Membership for the year was confirmed at 75, and the Library contained over 2000 slides and prints.

The decade that covers the life of the PhotoGroup has witnessed its strong growth to maturity. It has become an important specialist constituent Group in the Society, and has connections with other Groups, to the mutual advantage of all.

As this book was due at the printers, the death of John Wellsman was announced.

AT THE CENTRE: CHRISTINE PRESTON, ADMINISTRATOR

As the size and breadth of activities in the Society have grown, so has the need for more administrative assistance at its heart, especially for officers and group leaders. The Society has not always been able to pay for this assistance, and in earlier times, it was voluntary, and each activity had to find its own secretarial assistance. Indeed, this is still so today, but more and more there has been the need to provide certain equipment and services for all to use.

Christine Adnitt occupied the part-time post of Assistant General Secretary for a number of years until 1990, when expansion of her other professional job necessitated her resignation. She typed much correspondence, took minutes and arranged EC meetings, circulated notices and information, and helped organize the magazine delivery system. In her time, many people at the top of the Society were still employed and Christine's assistance was vital. She was assisted by Janet Davis, who helped with letter and report writing, minute taking, particularly at the AGM, and she managed all the typing for the magazine for Cic Upcott when she first became Editor.

Christine Preston was appointed Assistant General Secretary in 1990; she was seeking a part-time job to fit in with her family commitments, and have the advantage of working from home. She was attracted to the task because of her education and professional training that brought together an interest in archaeology and the Classics, and the skills of word processing and clerical administration. The hands-on exploratory experiences of the first, the reflective qualities of the second, and the practical application of the third of this portfolio made her a first-class candidate for the post.

As required, she was home-based at the outset, appointed for 18 to 20 hours per week although, she recalls, the demands of the work often exceeded that and, she remembers wryly, there were calls at all hours, and even on Christmas Day!

"Did you mind that?" "Well, obviously yes, but not resent it; people were anxious and volunteers do not readily conform to the patterns of routine business processes. It went with the job…a bit like living over the shop."

Christine, like her predecessor, spent a number of years working from her converted dining room in Chesham. The town was convenient for many, and her welcome always ready – while not an ideal situation, there were attractions to being in her home with young children, to offset against the distractions of an 'Open all Hours' scenario, day and night. The administration was moved to the White Hill Centre in Chesham in late 2000, and Christine's home could become just that once more.

The new larger Office is a busy place, with all the paraphernalia of a modern office. It is the hub of the Society's business, and the place to which all initial enquiries are directed. Calls range from questions and answers more typical of a Chief Executive's office in a major corporation, to a member asking about his subscription. Small group and sub-committee meetings may have to be clerked, and minutes typed and dispatched. Today, there is more essential office routine than when Christine began; the membership is much larger, from around 4,000 when she began to about 7,500 now, in 2003. On the day of our discussion, 30 new applications had been received, to each of whom must be dispatched a new member's pack, complete with information about the Society, and an invitation to join in, and fill in a survey form.

The increased workload has meant that other paid part-time assistants, including Helen Nolan until 2002, Trish Lennie and Lyn Curthoys, and some volunteers have been brought in to help. These new arrangements mean that there are other colleagues in support, attending to specific tasks, combining together when a rush job is necessary, sharing the work and each taking and running with a task as the demands and pressures fluctuate and change. "And," Christine adds, "the relief now, to be rid of the guilty feeling when returning from holiday to find a mass of post awaiting attention."

"Busy office; that could imply other pressures?"

"Yes, but I like a challenge. We were immensely challenged with the Society's Millennium Project, the Chiltern Way. Appeal letters had to circulated, and responses processed; the celebration of its launch and the administration that went with it required a great deal of extra work, with all the hundred and one things that attach to an event of that size and caliber. Then we had the work connected with the Membership Survey, involving new computer and dedicated database, which needed special training to manage. That was an enormous job.

"More recently, we had the Direct Debit promotion, the outcome of a special appeal to members so that we could make our financial status more stable. There were time scales and targets to be met, letters to go out, answers to process and proper records to maintain. We are now a company limited by guarantee and the Charity Commissioners require us to be very meticulous in the way our business is handled. The challenge to achieve this, as with the Millennium Project, was stimulating and enjoyable. I like a challenge of that sort.

"The new office accommodation is a happy place in which to work. The atmosphere is relaxed, and spacious enough and responsive to circumstances that may be demanding. We can use our modern technology to advantage and have been able to develop our use of computers. These things are critical given the pace of the Society's recent growth."

Does Christine see, viewing from the vantage point of the administration, the Society moving forward?

She is very aware of the problem common to many contemporary voluntary groups and organizations: active, participatory membership is coming from a more middle-aged and older group of people than 20 years ago. She feels the Society is positively attracting new members, but that not quite meeting the target of a broader age range, appealing to families, to younger generations.

In a sense, she echoes what Michael Rush, the immediate past Chairman had been saying to Annual Meetings: there is a need to engage with the new members and different social groups. The initiation of the Cyclegroup recently is one example; the introduction of family group walks is another.

Since the Government reforms in the 1980s of the rules governing charities, there has been a growing public expectation of immediacy of response that can be extremely difficult, unless the organization is in the truly big league. Public demand does not differentiate between national, regional and local in this context. This can be a problem for many administrators of medium-sized charities of which the Chiltern Society is one.

Christine has enjoyed her Administrator's role, the title changed in the late 90s to fit more exactly with her growing role. The contact with people is one of the attractions

Enterprise: The Mail Order Bookshop and Mobile Sales Team

The Mail Order Bookshop and the Mobile Sales Team have been valued features in the Society's support services for several years; in earlier years the Society was grateful for the profits from the Shop to help it survive, and there have been a number of dedicated organisers of this activity. Home made jams, cakes, coasters, notepads, tea towels and other popular items were regularly displayed, and there was always a good selection of cards, calendars, and other seasonal goods available.

After a short period when only Cic Upcott and Edward Newmark took stock to meetings and events, in 1998 Norman Joyce was appointed manager and buyer and set about trying to significantly increase business by broadening the stock offer, and structuring attendance at local shows, regional events, and conferences.

In the two and a quarter years following his appointment Norman successfully increased the Bookshop's income by over 800%. Sales fell during 2001 as the result of the Foot and Mouth closure of the countryside but by the end of 2002, the upward trend had resumed, reflecting also the enlarging Society membership.

The Bookshop's book and map catalogue today parallels the interests and demands of its customers. Among the 50 titles are walks and cycling guidebooks to suit family, weekend and mid-week walkers, and long-distance enthusiasts and groups. Most books specialise in the Chilterns, although the D'Arcy Dalton Way by Nick Moon features circular walks in the Oxfordshire Cotswolds and the Thames Valley.

Likewise the catalogue caters for interests in local (Chiltern) history, offering Richard Whitmore's celebration in words and pictures of the late Queen Mother's home countryside in and around St Paul's Waldenbury. Special interests include books about Chiltern lost railways, and Thames Valley airfields in World War Two, and Chiltern videos.

The Society's own publications are generally available: maps, videos about the Society and the Chilterns, major publications like *Treasures of the Chilterns*, written by members and compiled by Tony Hyde, Ken Poyton, and Cic Upcott.

The most popular sales from the Mail Order Bookshop and the MST included Nick Moon's fine guidebook to the Society's Millennium Project, The Chiltern Way. Orders received through the post are normally responded to within seven days. Norman Joyce made it a practice to keep in regular touch with appropriate publishers to ensure that the Bookshop continues to offer the latest published volumes that touch the features and character of the Chiltern country.

Norman has been ably and enthusiastically supported by Helen Preece who, in 2000, shared the task of running the Mobile Sales Team (MST) and took over full co-ordinating responsibility in 2001. She increased the number of events attended annually to 16, rising to 24 during the next two years. The shop stocks badges, greetings cards and Christmas cards in season.

Helen has recruited a team of 21 helpers to assist at various events throughout the year. All are volunteers, each one averaging about three show attendances per year; training was given to the first recruits by Dave Howarth, significantly adding to their skills in selling both goods and memberships. Sometimes they are retired, but often members are attracted by an activity which is in contrast to their day-to-day work life. Deciding which regional events to visit has to be planned well in advance, having regard to personal commitment. There are annual events that MST attends regularly; new ones each year, often included as the result of invitations received at shows. The large County Shows tend to prove costly; charges for pitch hire are usually high; sales and membership returns, low.

The best locations are those local events dedicated to a particular purpose; thus, in 2003, the 24 scheduled visits include Long Marston's Village Day, Live Crafts and other fairs at COAM, Kensworth Fun Day, Ashridge Centre (National Trust), and Monks Risborough Horticultural Show. These also reveal growing evidence of the Society's higher public profile. Helen says:

"When I first started, common questions were 'Who are you?', 'What do you do?' Today, people are much more likely to know who we are, to comment on the work we do – for instance, footpath clearance – and, if they are not already in membership, to join."

Progress and development in the Bookshop has been matched by a steady increase in activity, variety of locations, number of visits each year, achieved by the Mobile Sales Team since 1999. Both areas of information support have brought benefits to the Society through increasing the membership, raising the profile (as Norman says: "showing the flag"!), and providing an income.

INDEPENDENT INCORPORATED PARTNERS IN THE CHILTERN SOCIETY'S HISTORY

CHILTERN OPEN AIR MUSEUM (COAM) from original research by Howard Gilbert and augmented by Cic Upcott and Museum staff

The Museum was proposed to the Chiltern Society Executive Council as an appropriate project to celebrate European Architectural Heritage Year in 1975. The proposition reflected a key interest and commitment of the Society's Historic Works and Buildings Group (HWBG): how best to conserve the Chiltern heritage of fine farm buildings, and rescue a representative selection from demolition. John Willson, founder member of the Society, had visited the Weald and Downland Open Air Museum at Singleton in 1973, and his enthusiasm proved to be infectious.

"The germ of the idea for a museum of local buildings grew out of meetings of the Historic Works and Buildings Group ... under Dick Amsden's chairmanship, and of informal discussions in the Red Lion afterwards. But it was largely Dick and Joan's determination and hard work that made it possible."

The words are from a short obituary in *Chiltern News* following the sudden death of Joan Amsden (Dick's wife and Co-Director) that occurred on 20 May 1984. In the next year, a reconstructed barn from Hill Farm, Chalfont St Giles, was dedicated to Joan's memory. Tim Amsden carried out the flint walling and roof tiling, and Christopher Wallis carried out essential repair and construction work.

Don Gresswell took a keen interest in the Museum. In 1977 he donated £5,000 to facilitate the development at a critical moment, keeping in regular touch with its progress and he gave another £1,000 to fund the first guidebook.

Enquiries were made of Buckinghamshire, Hertfordshire and Oxfordshire County Councils, about their interest and possible sites. Bucks requested its land agent to look for suitable sites on the "London" side of the County. After viewing several, including places in private ownership, the Steering Committee secured an understanding for a 25-acre site at Newland Park, Chalfont St.Giles.

COAM was given Tenant-at-Will status by the County Council but, as Dick Amsden wrote later:

"... we had no lease and did not exist as an entity". He continues: "1978 and 1979 were years of great activity. ... Building and site work were intense, despite the fact that we still had no lease, (although by October 1978 we had been given official permission to erect buildings, again at our own risk!).

"Plans were afoot for a massive fund-raising activity."

Just under two years later the Council granted a 99-year lease. Finally COAM opened its doors to the public on 3 May 1981. Growth has been remarkable since the first day. There are many more exhibits and this greater diversity of buildings forms the basis from which a lively, active public agenda and an education programme for schools has emerged.

Professional staff

In 1986 moves were made to secure a full-time professional director to run the Museum. Next year James Moir and his wife Miriam were appointed joint Directors. The Museum has now a new professional Director, an Education Officer, a Buildings Manager, a Site and Farm Manager, and a Marketing Manager, assisted when necessary by paid (part-time) Interpreters. Much of the day-to-day running of the site, whether open or not, is carried out by some 200 volunteer helpers, and there is much support by a volunteer Friends of the Open Air Museum organisation.

The Buildings

Joanna Ruddock, the Director since March 2001, has described something of the Museum's attractiveness.

"In 25 years since the Museum's foundation, much has been achieved. We now have over 30 historic buildings re-erected on our 45-acre site ... Exhibits range from an early 16th century barn to a complete farmyard dating from the Victorian period, and a 1940s pre-fab. We also have a number of historic buildings from around the Chilterns, in store awaiting funds for their reconstruction."

The visiting public learn that

"... the Centre is a base for an exciting programme of cross-curricular environmental activities, delving into the many habitats on the Museum's 45-acre site." (Promotional leaflet)

Buildings are as varied as the corrugated iron chapel or mission room, of late Victorian times, from Henton in Oxfordshire, donated and restored during the mid-1990s, the Blythe Road Pavilion from Brook Green, Hammersmith, now used as the Museum's entrance and ticket office and shop, another pavilion from Maidenhead housing the Friends Centre, and the Museum administration in Astleham Manor Cottage, brought from a site close to Queen Mary Reservoir, Staines. Substantial financial help for transfer and reconstruction work on this cottage came from Thames Water. "Pat Lapham (was) Master Builder, " with many other volunteers helping.

The Wycombe Toll Booth is a central building, and there is an Apple Store from the former Leavesden Hospital, and a Cattle Byre from Borehamwood. Two City of London coal (and wine) payable duty boundary posts from Uxbridge, some cottage privies, and a Giles Gilbert Scott designed red telephone box, are among the fascinating exhibits.

Education Services

Two Sandford Awards for Excellence, (1994 and 1999) were made by the Heritage Education Trust, an independent body whose Trust Deed defines their objective as:

"The advancement of the education of the public in general and young people in particular in history and architecture and other environmental subjects through the study of historic buildings, their contents and surroundings and historic landscapes."

The Museum's Education Officer in 2003, Melissa Maynard, arranges many programmes for visiting school parties from the Chilterns and well beyond. Study Days and Field Trips can be and are arranged also for students from Colleges and Institutes of Higher Education. There are many visiting adult groups keen to know more of the history of each building.

Awards and Achievements

The Museum has been successful in achieving awards. In 1994 a research programme into thatching was secured, followed in 1995 by a national seminar on the results. COAM received one of the five 1997 Age Resource Awards of £1,000, sponsored by Unigate and administered by Age Concern England.

A remarkable award, London and Home Counties Loo of the Year 1992, was made following the reconstruction of the 1906 Caversham Public Conveniences donated by Reading Borough Council. The entire building, outer shell, cupola and pinnacle, consists of decorative tracery cast-iron panels, and large filligree pieces, making a building of prominence and distinction. Buildings Manager John Hyde-Trutch and many volunteers carried out the repair and reconstruction.

Programme growth

Presenting a lively annual programme of events, attractive to adults and children alike, has been the policy and staple of COAM since the day it opened.

In 1992 Chris Turner from Newham City Farm came to run the Victorian Farm. On arrival he found in residence five Light Sussex and two Red Dorking hens, and a cock; a pair of Greylag geese and three Golden Buff turkeys. Don Millar of the Chiltern Society's Conservation Volunteers had given them some months earlier. The farm has introduced goats, sheep and pigs since, the newborn lambs bringing visitors in numbers. Chris Turner was succeeded in 2000 by Nick Aylen, and Conway Rowland is the present Site and Farm Manager.

The Friends of COAM organise lectures, seminars and other events throughout the winter. In 1999 and again in 2001, the Museum site was used for the Chiltern Wood Festival, jointly organised by the Transnational Woodlands Industries Group (TWIG) and the Chiltern Woodlands Project Ltd. The professional organisation The Exhibition Team transformed this into a Live Crafts event. A popular dimension has now been added to attract new visitors, with the site being used by The Exhibition Team and other professional firms for their events, such as Homes and Gardens, and Food Festivals, and, a recent introduction, Noddy and Friends.

The Museum staff and volunteers continue to organise their own unique events, which have grown in number over the years. Some are designed especially for children, and some are timed to coincide with customary school holidays. Each Holiday Week offers hands-on activities within a particular theme, such as Easter Fun, Celtic and Mediaeval Weeks, Crafts, the 1940s, Victorian Week, and another with the interesting title of to Spooky Fun. Two four-day Weeks are, respectively, the Bodgers' Club, and Woodland Crafts. Children can join for just one day during a Week or any number of days, for the price of daily admission. These events are enjoyed by adults too, and Halloween and the Victorian Evening are very popular. Most popular visiting entertainers have been Lion Rampant, and Living Social History Network. Volunteers provide many of the teachers/leaders of these activities, from candle-making to wood-carving, and the traditional Father Christmas in season!

The Museum continues to attract families and interest groups, whether organised or informal, and to sharpen the emphasis upon heritage and personal social development through the ages.

Volunteers and voluntary effort
Crucial to the Museum's success are the volunteers who facilitate its smooth working. An insight into fascinating tasks which volunteers can do, including building construction and maintenance, is given by Joanna Ruddock in the article mentioned above.

"I have found that one of our greatest assets is our enthusiastic band of volunteers, who carry out a wide variety of tasks. These include building and site maintenance, staffing the shop, café, ticket counter and office as well as acting as stewards and interpreters of the buildings … our short-term priority is to concentrate our efforts on maintaining and enhancing what we have already in place. For example, we have over 5,000 artefacts, many of which are stored away. I want to give our visitors the opportunity to see more of these fascinating objects."

As national heritage centres and museums have found, many volunteers respond positively to taking roles from earlier generations. Beamish in the northeast, and Morwhellam in Cornwall are successful examples.

"We could develop a range of such activities appropriate to each of our exhibits as well as setting up teams of volunteers who might take responsibility for a particular building and work together to enhance our visitor's appreciation of its history and function."

A Company Limited by Guarantee
Archie Campbell (General Secretary of the Chiltern Society, 1975/81) stated that COAM had:

"... achieved birth, adolescence, majority and independence with great rapidity, thanks to the enormous amount of voluntary work ..."

The venture was quickly registered as a Company Limited by Guarantee to secure its charitable position.

The first Management Board comprised entirely Chiltern Society members; later their representation was limited to two persons from the Executive Council. Links were strengthened in 1991,when Society Chairman Harry Cook joined the Board, after a period of years with no Society link. Derek Upcott, Vice Chairman of the Chiltern Society, took on this role, and is now Chairman of COAM. Contact with the Historic Works and Buildings Group has been renewed.

CHILTERN WOODLANDS PROJECT (CWP)

This Project grew out of the Chiltern Society's Small Woodlands Project, set up in 1983 as a Community Programme funded by the Manpower Services Commission (MSC) to train unemployed people in woodland work; John Morris was employed as manager. Its early history to c1989 is outlined in Volume III of the Chiltern Society's story, written by Charles Mills whose initiative established the Project.

The MSC programme ended in September 1988. To separate the Project's finances from those of its founder, the Project became an independent non-profit making company limited by guarantee. In 1989 it was renamed *The Chiltern Woodlands Project Ltd* (CWP) and obtained charitable status in April 1991. Charles Mills chaired the Board during its first year, and briefly in 1993/94. In 1992 CWP was re-organised to become an advisory and consultative body with John Morris as manager and Peter Whipp as assistant manager.

The Project in 2001/02 - the Chairman's Report

In the Annual Report the Chairman, Buckinghamshire County Councillor Mrs Cherry Aston recalls some of the Project's achievements during that year. Despite extensive delayed access restrictions caused by the Foot and Mouth epidemic, Chiltern Woodlands Project managed a near normal number of woodland advisory visits. The Chilterns were linked with regions in Germany and Greece in a European Union funded, international partnership to research problems of declining woodland economies.

Her Report also draws attention to the valuable, continuing core work of the Project: giving advice to owners of unmanaged woodland, and where appropriate, helping them obtain grant support from the Forestry Commission's Woodland Grant Scheme. Woodland surveys to facilitate improved management, or identify archaeological features, were (and are) part of the Project's regular work during the year.

Each year the Project works in partnership with organisations and individuals. This Annual

Report records three examples: tree advice to the Chilterns Conservation Board's Chalk Streams project (CCCP); woodland surveys for the Woodland Trust, and the continuing management of the Chiltern Society's Bottom Wood.

An aim of CWP is to raise public interest and awareness of woodlands. The Year's work on this important aspect is noted and repeated in *The Chiltern Woods are Special*, a leaflet produced in 2001 with funding from the Ernest Cook Trust and Laing's Charitable Trust. The importance of control to reduce damage by grey squirrels and deer is instanced. Finally the organisation of seminars, short practical courses and workshops, lectures to specialised groups, and visits, are reported. Each one is part of the Project's annual work programme.

Finally Councillor Aston's review acknowledges the support received from the Project's partners. These include the Chilterns Conservation Board, Hertfordshire and Buckinghamshire County Councils; Aylesbury Vale, Chiltern, South Oxfordshire, Three Rivers and Wycombe District Councils, the Chiltern Society, the Ernest Cook Trust, Laing's Charitable Trust and the Countryside Agency.

The Project's Aims

Following a careful assessment of future strategy, a new Business Plan was approved recently by the Board of Directors. It is intended to guide the Project's work until 2005. The aims were re-defined:

- To promote and encourage the sustainable management of woodlands in the Chiltern Hills,
- to protect and enhance the landscape of the Chiltern Hills,
- to maintain and enhance the biodiversity of the Chiltern Hills.
- To promote a sustainable woodland economy.
- To promote awareness, understanding and enjoyment of the Chiltern woods.

CWP is dedicated to these aims; it is independent and able to listen to woodland owners' requirements whilst exploring various options, regulations on felling, grant availability, local policies and features of interest that affect woodland management.

Its focus is upon woodlands that are less than ten hectares (25 acres) although some larger unmanaged woods are visited. In practice the average area advised upon has been about four hectares.

The achievements between 1989 and 2003 have been substantial; apart from the continuing organising and event programmes, John Morris reports consultative visits to:

"485 small woodlands covering about 1850 hectares (4,540 acres) to offer advice on woodland management and to help owners appreciate the importance of their work for its flora and fauna, landscape, recreation and history."

Transition over time

The 1989 transition from a direct labour organisation to one offering an enlarged consultative role clearly extended the range and influence of the Project. The change came at a time of shrinking Government grant aid to ancilliary public services, and an increased pressure upon agencies through which funds were often channelled.

Following the conclusion of the Government-funded MSC Scheme, in 1992 District and County Councils in the AONB, who had financed part of the Project, reviewed the situation and decided to support the consultative, advisory and information services offered. Their decision, and that of other agencies and authorities, and the Chiltern Society has enabled the continued development of the Project and its subsequent 11 years of successful operation.

The situation was eased further by a three-year 'pump priming' grant from the Countryside Commission to sustain the assistant project manager's post. This ended in 1995 and the postholder, Peter Whipp was made redundant eighteen months later in September 1996 due to lack of funds. However, Peter was able to form his own working company, *Ridgeway Woodlands*, and because of his knowledge and experience, continues to give practical help to woodland owners in implementing the Project's management plans.

Re-location to Piggotts, North Dean, and archaeological studies

In the same year, the office was moved to Piggotts Wood, the owner, Nick Wheeler-Robinson generously offering to provide a room. John Morris, and Ken Westwood, the company secretary and part-time assistant, transferred there. The move proved advantageous in several ways. In particular it enabled John to engage in a detailed study of the history and archaeology of the Wood, building upon comparable work in the Chiltern Society's Bottom Wood. The discoveries were such that a training day was organised in November 1998 to illustrate features common to many other Chiltern small woodlands. Two Buckinghamshire woods, owned by the Woodland Trust have been similarly surveyed and sketch-mapped.

In the foreword to John's short book, *History in Chiltern Woods*, the Chiltern Society's President, Sir Leonard Figg wrote:

"John Morris has produced a most interesting and useful example of what an intelligent archaeological study can reveal in the Chiltern woods. For the woodland manager he rightly calls attention to the care which must be taken to respect archaeological features in the woods when conducting woodland management."

These features are the 'lumps and bumps' which turn out to be old sawpits, charcoal hearths, quarries and boundary banks, and they are to be found in many other ancient Chiltern woods, as well as elsewhere.

European research support for small woodlands (TWIG)

In 1999 the Project received a boost from participation in a European Union research scheme, the Trans-national Woodland Industries Group (TWIG). Participants came from the Chilterns, from two German regions, Trier and Thuringen, and from North Evia in Greece. These regions have problems of declining woodland economies; TWIG was the framework that enabled partners to meet, exchange experiences and ideas, arrange a series of seminars and events and undertake research to develop fresh management practices. *A Guide to Good Practice* was published in 2002 at the end of the programme.

TWIG's Steering Group was chaired by Steve Rodrick, the AONB Officer, with 12 participating partners including the Chiltern Woodlands Project. The Countryside Agency, and Buckinghamshire County Council provided extra funds to enable CWP to employ Mike Furness as TWIG's manager in the Chilterns.

In TWIG's Annual Report for 2000/01, Mike chronicled the useful part played by the Chiltern Woodlands Project in organising 58 successful woodland visits before the Foot and Mouth epidemic halted all such activity. CWP also arranged two major promotional events for TWIG., *Woods at Work*, held in Wendover Woods with the Forestry Commission, and the *Chiltern Wood Festival* sited at the Chiltern Open Air Museum. Each event was presented twice during the three years of the TWIG project.

All four of these TWIG events were made possible by the appointment of an assistant project manager to the Chiltern Woodlands Project, thanks to funding from the Countryside Agency. First, Loren Eldred held this post and was responsible for organisation and planning some of the events. Loren left during the winter 2001/02 on appointment to the National Trails Office in Oxfordshire. Graham Thorne succeeded him until the end of the TWIG project in June 2002.

The Board

Charles Mills, the Project's founder was succeeded by John Stidworthy, Chairman of the Trees and Woodlands Group of the Chiltern Society. John retired in 1994, to devote more time to the Bottom Wood Group. His successor, Jim Walker, remained in the Chair until 2001 when he stood down and County Councillor Mrs Cherry Aston of Bucks was elected. Jim continued to be a Board member and Vice-Chairman, with responsibility for finance. Other Directors included three from the Chiltern Society, and one each from the district councils of Aylesbury Vale, Chiltern District, South Bucks, South Oxfordshire, Three Rivers (Hertfordshire), and Wycombe.

Publicity

The Chiltern Woodlands Project has published a number of relevant short books on the work of Woodland management and its history; a lively newsletter is produced twice a year; display boards are permanently situated at the new Environment Centre in High Wycombe, and at the Chiltern Open Air Museum. A generous donation from the Fulmer Night Group, and another from the Ernest Cook Trust, in 2002, helped to fund the board updating and replacement.

Perspective on the Chiltern Woodlands Project

The Project's continuing vitality, relevance, and established value are a reflection of the energy, enthusiasm and dedication that the manager, John Morris, has brought to the job since Charles Mills appointed him in August 1983. He currently Chairs two highly relevant bodies, the Small Woods Association, and the Bucks and Oxfordshire division of the Royal Forestry Society.

Charles Mills, originator of the Chilterns Small Woodlands Project and its transition into CWP Ltd, died in November 1997. He was a Vice-President of the Chiltern Society to which he had devoted much of his recreational time in retirement since 1978, when he joined its Executive Council. In his obituary notice in *Chiltern News* John Morris paid tribute to him:

"(For the first five years) Charles was very closely involved, on a weekly basis, controlling the policy and finances of the Small Woodlands Project. In (September) 1988 the Community Programme came to an end. Charles worked hard to ensure that the work we had started would continue. And, with support from the Chiltern Society, local councils and the Countryside Commission, the Chiltern Woodlands Project was formed.

"(Charles) enjoyed getting out into the woods for site visits and occasionally helped the Bottom Wood Group with work, such as coppicing the hazel hedge below Toothill.

"In 1995 he produced Volume III of *The Chiltern Society Story* which reviewed 11 years work of the Society (1982-1992). This was an especially remarkable achievement because he managed to write this detailed account ... after his eyesight had failed and he had to learn to use a Braille typewriter. ... At the Project's AGM last September (1997) it was agreed he should be asked to become its first Patron and he was pleased to accept. His friendship, advice and support will be sadly missed."

The Chiltern Woodlands 20 successful years are a tribute to the enthusiasm, thought, care, and genius of this former senior civil servant and Chiltern Society Vice-President. He fostered the growth of the Society's membership, reformed the administration and created the circumstances in which both the Society and the Chiltern Woodlands Project developed.

PEOPLE MAKING A DIFFERENCE

Women contributors to the contemporary Chiltern Society

CHRISTINE BREDEN is the co-ordinator of the Society's Mid-Chilterns Conservation Volunteers one of the three separate divisions of the CCV. Christine joined the Society about

15 years ago soon after meeting the late Joan Herbert, a dedicated member of the Society and a Guide at the Chiltern Open Air Museum. Christine "...became interested..." in both COAM and the Chiltern Society.

In 1991 she started to work regularly with the CCV under Don Millar, and found herself taking part in village pond and green clearance, the maintenance of Chiltern special features like the Bledlow Cross, a task shared with the HWBG, or bramble clearance and hedge encroachment control as in recent work at Seer Green, in Buckinghamshire.

Seven years or so ago, around 1996/7, when the then Group Secretary had to relinquish the job, Christine stepped into her place, now being named the Co-ordinator. Since then she has:

"become more involved in planning the activities and sometimes organising and running the events ..."

That role has intensified following the tragic death of Don Millar in January 2002. This was a great shock to the Group, to the Society, and to all who knew him, including Christine herself who had worked with him for so long.

Don had organised the work of conservation volunteering, taking over in 1986 from the late Don Gresswell. As the work became more Chiltern-wide, Don had re-organised the Group to manage it, and Christine took charge of the central area and is now heading and developing its programme. This was not a straightforward task of 'just collecting the trailer and the tools', as she explains:

"When Don Millar died ... I took over the week-end Mid-Chilterns group and have had to pick up from there; the deaths of both my parents, and all the essential family business which that entailed, combined with this new responsibility, made 2002 a difficult one for us all. Now we have a new schedule and we have resumed our regular, monthly Saturday meetings."

The task is substantial but her commitment has continued because she is a person who is passionate about the living environment and its rich diversity. Witness to this is how she complements her Chiltern Society work with strong support for the Royal Society for the Protection of Birds (RSPB), the Wildlife Wetlands Trust, and the enthusiastic way in which she talks about bird watching expeditions to Welney in Norfolk, and sanctuaries like Bass Rock, St. Kilda, and Islay in the Western Isles. Her description of a sea voyage from Plymouth to the Mull of Kintyre, and the viewing of colonies of skua and sheerwater at breeding time confirms her deep interest in conservation, and why one of her main concerns in working with the Mid-Chilterns Group is the maintenance of habitat for the wildlife of the AONB.

Why does she do it? What motivates her? What personal gain is there in doing what she does? Surely there has to be more to it than just the satisfaction of 'being useful'? This is how she feels about it.

"I have been to and seen a lot of new places that I would not have been to but for the ConsVols' work and events. And then there are the people who so enjoy coming out to do the work and make a contribution however small or large; this is the enjoyment that we all have, and the bonus is the characters that we meet.

"It has been particularly rewarding when we have helped other small community groups, who just need a bit of support to get going; using our robust tools, and working with our people who already have that confidence to do things, motivates them to bigger and better activities.

"The Chiltern Society can give these small groups support to do their own thing, and get their small piece of the Chilterns restored, or make it more accessible to the local people who use it."

Did her career training help her in what she does for CCV?

"No; my profession is Facilities Manager in the building maintenance industry which is not related to conservation. Working with Don Millar you were trained by practice and experience. I am still working a full-time 5-day week, and manage the voluntary job and other things at the weekend. For instance, I have two beautiful Dalmation dogs; one is liver-spotted and therefore very special. We show them in various parts of the country, and recently achieved an Award, second in their Class, at Crufts."

What are her most treasured recollections?

"People's thanks for the help, physical and advisory, once they, and we see the impact the project has had on them, as people, and on the environment and location that has been restored."

A quiet hint of those 'treasured recollections' is contained in the programme summary Christine wrote for the September 2001 edition of *Chiltern News*.

"**Saturday 23 October:** A return visit to the lovely Mrs Mack at Aston Clinton to clear Bear Brook (at Home Farm) of watercress growth …"

Mrs Mack is the owner of the house and garden abutting onto the farm field through which the Bear Brook flows. She is a Society member and one of the large team of helpers who used to distribute *Chiltern News* four times a year. ConsVols' periodic visit to clear the Brook is an occasion when she is in contact with other members, provides lunch for the team, and welcomes them to her home, and the visit is always eagerly anticipated by all.

Another remembered champagne moment was forecast during the same season before Christmas 2001. The occasion was visiting a well-loved spot that looks across the wide plain of the Oxfordshire countryside to where she lives, but enjoying once again that spectacle seen from the top of the escarpment in late autumn. Allied to this the pleasure of working alongside others from the Society's Historic Works and Buildings Group.

"**Saturday 8 December:** Our annual visit to Bledlow Ridge and the Chalk Cross to clear scrub and tidy up after the summer and autumn. We should be joined by members of the Historic Works and Buildings Group as well, who are responsible for this ancient monument."

The Chiltern Society has many members who, like Christine, work voluntarily in the field, regularly, year on year, quietly dedicated to the task of sustaining the Chilterns as an area of outstanding natural beauty.

BERYL HUNT joined Rights of Way Group walks led by Dr Leslie Drain in Oxfordshire, two or three years before she became a full member of the Chiltern Society. In 1990 she registered her interest more formally in these areas: Historic buildings, Trees, Hedgerows and Woodlands; Conservation. Don Millar recruited her to help extend the activities of the Conservation Volunteers into South Oxfordshire. Beryl agreed to help.

She has maintained a lifelong interest in the environment and conservation; during her childhood she went walking and cycling in the countryside with her father. He had a keen interest in the natural environment and identified for her many of its fascinating features, the bird life, flora, and the shape of and buildings in the landscape. As a result, she has always had an interest in wildlife and in the history of the area where she lives.

Her development of practical skills in both pottery and ceramics led her into teaching adults at leisure. Appreciating and enjoying this commitment she decided to become a trained teacher, and entered college as a "very mature student specialising in Geography with a particular interest in Environmental Studies". This enabled her to focus her understanding of the environment and provided frames of reference for the conservation work to which she is devoted. She was therefore able to respond positively to the contact made by Don Millar.

Don asked her to look at Widmore Pond on Sonning Common and to give an opinion on its condition; she did so and wrote survey report for him, on which future action could be based. She then agreed to try and set up a Volunteer group in the South Chilterns, on the condition that she would not do so single-handed.

"Don found Ken Smith who had recently left the police service and was keen to help. Ken and I seemed to complement each other and we worked together for 5 or 6 years until the demands of his job forced him to give up. Roger Watson has now succeeded to Ken's role.

"We set up the South Chilterns (Conservation) Volunteers (SCV) and I think we were a good team. 'Conservation' was dropped from our title later to reflect the fact that we were taking on work in industrial archaeology and structures, not just nature conservation. This wide variety of sites and work has helped to form a loyal and dedicated volunteer group.

"My work then (and now) included surveying sites and giving advice. This ranged from answering a 'phone query to providing a full-scale management plan. Don frequently asked my advice on ponds throughout the Chilterns, on which the work would then be done by the Central Volunteers Group. To widen my experience I attended various day and week-end courses and now attend the South Oxfordshire Countryside Forum."

Captain Harry Cook, who chaired the Society from 1988 to 1993, sought to promote Support and Information Groups (SIGs) as a vehicle for extending and locally focusing the organisation's work and membership. Beryl, assisted by Michael Wyatt, tried to establish a South Oxfordshire Group.

The attempt began with a lecture series given by Professor Oliver Rackham, an historical ecologist from Cambridge University, Stephen Crowe, Chief Planning Officer for England and Wales and other eminent speakers. Beryl comments:

"These were very much formal lectures followed by questions and gave no opportunity for members to get to know each other which was Harry Cook's aim for the Groups."

The effort was not wholly successful at the time. In 1994 they tried to re-invigorate the South Chiltern S & I Group that had been formed. Several meetings were organised, plus a coach trip to the Chiltern Open Air Museum; but only Nigel Snell, the *Red Kite Man* was a "real crowd puller" and thereafter it did not prove possible to find sufficient people to sustain the organising base necessary for a strong group. Harry Cook tried to persuade Beryl to join the Executive Council and help the Groups to develop. She declined, but suggested that her husband, Hugh, would be a better committee member.

In1992 the SCV, led by Beryl and Ken Smith, began work on the recovery of the Ewelme Watercress Beds, continued with help from the Friends, and the Sonning Common Green Gym. The Friends of Ewelme Watercress Beds was formed in 1995 to target local interest on the possibility of purchasing the Beds. As instigator of the rescue programme, Desmond Dix was the natural Chairman.There followed three and a half years of intricate, difficult exploration and negotiation during which one of the Beds' joint-owners died, and contact with his partner was achieved only at irregular intervals. Site work was suspended while discussions and exchanges continued. Beryl, the Friends, and their supporters persisted and succeeded. She writes:

"By September 1999, following much preparation, an Appeal was launched by Jeremy Irons for £125,000 to buy the Beds and carry out the necessary repairs. In less than six months £145,000 was raised and in November 2000, the purchase was completed. Work re-started immediately. A management committee was formed with representatives from the Parish Council, the Ewelme Society and the Friends of the Watercress Beds, together with two specialist advisers and representation from the Chiltern Society."

Alongside this, SCV continued its varied programme. During the 11 years to 2001, Beryl led the Group into 20 major conservation and restoration projects. In many, as with the Ewelme Watercress Beds, she has fostered partnerships with organisations as various as the Sue Ryder Retreat House, the Huntercombe Golf Club, the Disabled Drivers' Association, and the Castle Venture Scout Group. This local identification with the work is something in which she believes passionately. Equally she has a strong feeling for the Chilterns as a whole, as a rich and precious area of chalkland in southern England.

What are the rewards in this active commitment to conservation?

Beryl identifies a number of high points since she began in 1990. The heather regeneration project at Nettlebed and District Commons: "Hard work but very rewarding". The restoration of Highmoor Pond near Henley-on-Thames: "a seven-year unremitting task". The reconstruction of the Victorian Water Tank at Bix, completed in time for the Bix and Assenden Golden Jubilee Celebrations.

On a more personal level, the receipt in 1999 of the Natural Pioneers' Millennium Award of £1,285 for the purchase of a video recorder as a "site recording tool" was a highlight. (The donors were British Conservation Trust for Volunteers and the Millennium Commission.) Two years later an invitation came to Beryl and Hugh to attend a Buckingham Palace Garden Party.

Soon after, in 2001 a pleasing recognition of the Group came from Baroness Buscombe inviting 12 South Chiltern Volunteers to visit the House of Lords, attend a debate, and have tea in the Palace of Westminster.

What about a 'champagne' moment; an event or experience that was, and is the greatest moment during the past 12 years?

"Without question, the marvellous evening when, in August 2000, we celebrated to mark raising enough money to buy the Beds. 300 donors were present; our Guest of Honour was Hugo Brunner, Lord Lieutenant of Oxfordshire who had taken a personal interest in what we were trying to do."

Beryl has one other major commitment to which she gives time. She is a "… committee member responsible for planning matters for Goring and Streatley Amenity Association". Beyond this, Beryl Hunt is a member of the Berks, Bucks and Oxfordshire Wildlife Trust, the Project Officer for the Ewelme Watercress Beds and, since October 2002, an elected representative member of the Chiltern Society's Executive Council. And she adds: "I am supposed to be retired!"

CIC UPCOTT's connection with the Chiltern Society began in 1969, soon after she and her husband, Derek, became respectively, Secretary and Chairman of the Chesham Society. This is an active organisation, and then was much concerned with the increasing density of through traffic on the main street, causing congestion and greater risk to pedestrians. Founded eight years before the Chiltern Society, in 1957, this local group successfully focused residents' interests and concerns about the need for a solution, and on many other issues.

This brought Cic and Derek into closer touch with the Chiltern Society, which they were able to assist in many ways, and vice versa, also attending many of its social events and meeting many of its activists. The two organisations had much in common that, several years later, brought beneficial results for the latter.

In 1975 the newly formed Chesham and District Community Association purchased the White Hill School from Bucks County Council. The White Hill Centre then became a popular central location and meeting place for many local clubs and voluntary bodies. Cic was founder Chairman of the Association, whilst continuing as Secretary of the Chesham Society. She remembers:

"These activities and events were closely intertwined, helping to bring together people in the town who came to support more than one cause. … From the Centre's set-up the Chiltern Society made use of many of its facilities, including rooms for Council and Executive Committee meetings. The printed work for the Chiltern Society's Community Programme (the Small Woodlands Project) was produced in the Centre's Print Room. Minutes of meetings, occasional leaflets, and booklets about the Society's other projects were also printed. Chiltern Society members, Charles Mills particularly, were regularly at the Centre on Society business."

In the early months of 1988, Elizabeth Stacey, editor of the *Chiltern News* since 1981, resigned. Cic applied for the job and was appointed. She says:

"*Chiltern News* had arrived at my house because I was both a member, and Secretary of the Chesham Society. I had met some of the Society Editors over the years, and having always had a knowledge of and interest in printed matter, had started a newsletter called *Focus* for the Chesham Society, still going today!

"In the spring of 1988, with White Hill Centre going well, and my other activities under control – more or less – I saw a new Editor was needed for the Chiltern Society's magazine. I applied and got the job. This started a whole new era in my life; I joined the Executive Council, and began to find out how the Chiltern Society was run."

A year or two previously she had become active nationally as a member of the Community Association movement, chairing its Law Monitoring Committee. Captain Harry Cook had been elected as Chairman of the Chiltern Society soon after she joined the Executive Council, and his own declared plans to raise the image of the Society coincided with Cic's.

"I was able to use my experience and knowledge to help to begin shaping the CS into a more modern organization, happily supporting Harry Cook in his plans."

In her first issue of *Chiltern News* she indicated that she favoured some changes in future production and that she was investigating the possibility of computer-generated desk top publishing (DTP). Changes were introduced gradually.

"The magazine itself grew and grew; the black and white version remained in place and various means were used to produce the columns of text. A professional graphics designer, Andy Wilkinson, was eventually brought in; the day of DTP had arrived.

"This first period was a sharp learning curve, but as the Society grew and began to prosper, the idea of a colour magazine began to harden in my own mind, for use when the moment was right."

Cic believes that the Chairmanship of Harry Cook is one of the high points of the Society''s history and regards her:

"association with him, and several other similarly minded members, as occupying the best hours yet spent in the work of promoting the Society, both to its own members and to the outside world, which was somewhat uninformed of what the Society stood for and did."

Barry Scott, who succeeded Harry Cook, consolidated the changes that had been introduced by his predecessor, aided by Michael Rush as Vice-Chairman from 1995. When Michael became Chairman in 1997 he resumed the pace of change that Harry had set, by proposing even more reforms and innovative developments.

A Marketing Group was established, one of its tasks being to review the Society's public image. Cic found herself with a wider role, participating in many working groups and taking responsibility for more publications and material. Following professional advice, Michael persuaded the Executive Council to commission and adopt a new Society logo. This settled an outstanding issue; the new sign attracted much favourable comment although, for some, the loss of the pollarded beech was regretted. CWP has adopted it for its own logo.

Working first with Edward Newmark, Membership Secretary, and later with Peter Hawkes of Hawkes Design, Chesham, Cic provided new, attractive promotion leaflets which, when distributed around the Chilterns, began to encourage new membership applications and enquiries. However, the high point of the efforts was achieved in the autumn of 1998, when *Chiltern News* (No.149) was the first edition to be printed in colour, displaying the new logo for the first time to the membership. Other publications followed, particularly *Treasures of the Chilterns*, a good-looking booklet of 250 places of interest in the Chilterns, and the first new-look *Annual Report* designed by Glyn Kuhn for the Annual General Meeting in October 2000.

Improving the appearance of the magazine and developing its content has been a great pleasure to Cic. This creative role together with the introduction of new technological processes, and the digital camera add to her enjoyment of editorship.

One of her finest times, in recent years, was preparation for the Chiltern Society's Millennium Project, the Chiltern Way. Producing the appeals promotion leaflet proved quite a challenge:

"Dave Howarth did a great job reproducing the route on an Ordnance Survey backing albeit out of date, but floating this accurately onto our own screened map took many hours of work by Peter Hawkes, Rob Bethell following Nick Moon's guide, and me."

The appeal was successful, "funds poured in", and a second and third edition of the leaflet was necessarily produced.

The enthusiasm and energy that Cic Upcott has brought to the creation of the contemporary *Chiltern News* is apparent in every issue produced. Her commitment and involvement in the wider publications field is of equal measure. What she describes as a "small sideline" is the job of promoting the Society and its rich variety of activities through talks to clubs and groups the length and breadth of the Society area. The talks are a vehicle for informing non-members about what the Society does, as well as recruiting new members. She says the "what" even surprises those Society members present, so the work of spreading the word still needs to go on. "That's part of my enjoyment."

Was she trained for this?

"I had no actual training for this job, but went after school to art college, then to work in a large London library. Thereafter I worked in London County Council's Education Department with sites and buildings, a marvellous period for a frustrated architect. In all my jobs, journalistic or display or typographical skills were needed and had to be learned along the way. A love of amateur dramatics, designing stage sets and costumes, even writing pantomimes, and a complete inability to stop thinking up activities for others to enjoy has led me to the present."

Have there been real 'champagne moments'? Two stand out from Harry Cook's time.

"The first was the fact that Derek, my husband, working in Luton and Bedfordshire, met Michael Gwilliam soon after his appointment as Bedfordshire's Chief Planning Officer.

"Mike wanted to know more about the Chiltern Conference, then almost inactive. After an introductory meeting with me over a pre-match lunch at Luton Town football ground, we brought him together with Chairman Harry Cook, and so began a new era for this crucial AONB management body, culminating today in the Chilterns Conservation Board.

"The second event of significance was meeting the late Iain Drummond soon after he became Chairman of Chiltern Open Air Museum. ... His and my shared concerns at the lack of representation at Board level by the Society, the initial founding group, led to an introduction to Harry Cook, and his taking a place on that Board."

Cic Upcott is the longest serving Editor, in a line that includes the first Society pioneers, then Max Davies and Archie Campbell, and Liz Stacey her immediate predecessor, who is now a Chiltern District councillor.

Her husband, Derek is Chairman of the Chiltern Open Air Museum (COAM). He is also Vice-Chairman of the Chiltern Society. Both husband and wife are long established members of the Executive Council, each devoting many hours annually to the voluntary work that has inspired their lives for more than 40 years.

In an observation that typifies their contribution to the Society's work, and that of others who engage similarly, Cic remarks:

"Technically, I am well past retirement age, but so are many in the Society, and we give gladly of our time and energy in a variety of ways. This voluntary input is one of the things that make this Society so unique and, if I may say so, successful."

The Society's membership, almost doubled in the four years up to 2001, due in part to the success of new promotional material and its widespread distribution, and to *Chiltern News* continuing to raise awareness and communicating information about relevant contemporary issues. Cic thoroughly enjoys the fact that what she has contributed has, like so many of other volunteers' efforts, made quite a difference in how the Society functions and appeals to the public today.

Men making a difference

DAVE HOWARTH is Membership Secretary of the Chiltern Society having joined in the mid-80s whilst still working as a chemist with the public water services. He says that this role, and his residence in the Chilterns gave him a sense of the environment as an important priority in modern living. When water services were privatised, Dave joined Thames Water to manage a large West London works, subsequently directing and organising training. He took early retirement, formed his own consultancy and continued involvement in water services, travelling to Egypt on behalf of an Italian contracting company.

Meantime, on leave, he walked the Chiltern footpaths, preparing perhaps for the time when he linked up with the local ROWG programmes which he began to do during the mid-90s. In November 1998 he was elected to the Executive Council as a member representative; at about the same time he offered his help in any practical way within his capacity to Michael Rush. One outcome was the idea to create a Society video, and in this he could call on his training expertise in the use and presentation of visual material.

Dave teamed up with Reg Clarke, a Society member who offered his technical assistance, Dave applying himself to the script and film structure. Dave says for him, a 'champagne' occasion was the agreement of Susan Hampshire, also a member, to do the voice-over of the video. Michael Rush wrote the invitation, she responded with enthusiasm and the work was complete: the first ever video had been produced by members for members to promote the Society.

When Edward Newmark stood down in January 2000, Dave succeeded him as Membership Secretary in which post he remains. He has engaged in a careful review of recruitment processes; as a member of the Strategic Planning Team he led a small working group to develop a Membership Questionnaire, and review of the Society's data base. The early results were the identification of many members with skills and experience of value to the Society, and some increase in commitment. The introduction of Direct Debit payment supported this. He has initiated a network of leaflet distribution across the Chilterns, found Jenny and Geoff Kingsnorth as recruiters at large on behalf of the Society: "Some members may have seen them in Sainsburys in Chesham in January 2003".

As Membership Secretary he sees much advantage in the Society's non-political stance, one of its great strengths. He believes the development of new ways of interesting and holding members is an important part of the way forward. One idea came from a former Society Chairman and now Vice President Wing Commander Derek Martin OBE. Derek visited pubs in a wide circle around his home, spoke to landlords, and left packs of membership leaflets there for the customers. In a letter in October 2002 to Dave about his campaign he wrote:

"The membership campaign in pubs has been a great success. I have now left packs in 15 pubs, also leaving a copy of Chiltern News with the landlord, plus a copy of the relevant footpath map with the pub highlighted.

"Without exception, all landlords have welcomed the information. Many have said that it was just what was needed, but they did not know where to seek the information. Others said they were frequently asked for information about walks around their pub, and some have had the Society map mounted and hung in the bar."

Dave points out that the Society's voluntary status and independence are valuable benefits when dealing with business and commercial leisure interests, as well as with official bodies. Society independence is also a benefit when dealing with official bodies.

Apart from the video success of which he is very proud, he was absorbed in, and enthusiastic about the Chiltern Way project to which he contributed some of the publicity preparation. He gives much time and energy to the Society; he says he is someone who likes being involved in a multiplicity of activity; what does he get out of it?

"I had to learn how to become computer literate. When we started on the video my skills were relatively minimal. I had used a computer at work, but that was on a centrally controlled system; it gave me keyboard skill, but not the capacity to create. The video production was a sharp and valuable learning curve in the use of information technology. It fired my enthusiasm for modern communication methods; learning more about them I was able to encourage others in the Society to do the same.

"Soon after this, the idea was born for a full Chiltern Society website. A technology student at Buckinghamshire Chilterns University College offered to help and, between us we prepared and launched the Society's comprehensive first website, now managed by Colin Wells. I think one of the great things about the Society is the opportunity it gives for members to develop new skills and engage in learning. I like to be busy, and keep my mind active."

Dave is proud at having enabled the membership to grow; he aims to stabilise the base and see it increase toward the mid-decade target of 12,000. As part of a plan to carry this forward he designed the Small Business Support Scheme and the new Community Partners strategy for launch in mid-2003.

JOHN TAYLOR. Honorary Treasurers are special people, partly because their expertise, whilst not unique, is comparatively scarce in the voluntary sector. It can be a difficult, intricate job in any lively, active organisation because the demand for resources almost always outstrips the immediate capacity to satisfy them. The good treasurer has to encourage enterprise and initiative, yet maintain the balance of funds so that the organisation or society continues to grow and develop, enabling it to do what it wishes, while keeping the balance sheet 'in the black'. The Chiltern Society is extremely fortunate in its present post holder, in a long line of treasurers from earliest days.

John Taylor is dedicated to ensuring the best possible solutions for the Society's ambitious development plans. In 1999, 18 months after he took over the job and laid the foundations of a larger accounting system than he inherited, he proposed to raise £10,000 from the investment portfolio to facilitate the schemes just coming on line, some of which needed pump priming. Sufficient working capital was needed for the Marketing project, Ewelme Watercress Beds, and the Chiltern Way, for instance, until income returns began to balance expenditure. His decision to act this way was vindicated, and he was able to report to the 2001 AGM that income overall had risen from £76,000 to £180,000.

John is a Chartered Accountant and former company Finance Director. He, his wife, and family have lived in the Chilterns since 1968, and appreciate the quality of living in the Hills. He joined the Society some 20 years ago, and enjoys walking, both in the Chilterns and, with his wife, in southern France on holidays. On retirement from full-time working, he saw the advertisement in *Chiltern News*, and decided it was a way to "give something back to the community" in return for the many happy years spent in the Chilterns.

The desire to offer a return went a great deal further when he responded to Birmingham University's Cancer Research appeal, involving finding sponsors for a six-day 100km trek on the Great Wall of China to raise funds. Their son had earlier survived testicular cancer; this was the opportunity he had been looking for. In October 2001 he and 82 others set off on this adventure. On 18 October he wrote:

"I returned … just over a day ago, and am recuperating from bruised, shorter legs and lost pounds, but it has been a thoroughly exhilarating and demanding challenge that has required substantial reserves of determination to complete …83 people from all over the British Isles, young and old, male and female, virtually all covered the 100km of rough, uneven terrain, climbed 6000 feet of hills and walls, descended more or less safely, visited remote Chinese villages and endured some of the most primitive accommodation I have seen or experienced for over 20 years.

"For three days we walked in an area of the Great Wall some 130km from Beijing ... largely in its natural, un-renovated state. (The wall passage follows the contour of the land, and frequently becomes a series of long upward or downward rough stone stairways.) We ventured off the Wall through villages where men were riding well-kept donkeys, and women were washing clothes in the local stream and threshing corn by a manual method which I feel sure the Romans had automated some 2000 years ago."

The group raised some £200,000 for the Cancer project; John's part of this was £4,000, a fine personal achievement of which he is truly proud.

He is impressed with the breadth of activity and enthusiasm of Society members, and believes there is a great and continuing need for its work, particularly like that at Ewelme and on the Chiltern Way. He is proud of the cooperative effort the Society made to help raise funds to save ancient Penn Wood from housing development and a golf course, enabling its purchase by the Woodland Trust.

He is also glad of the efforts of Michael Rush, supported by the Executive Council, to establish a central administrative base at White Hill Centre, and believes this will enable the infinitely better deployment of the Society's resources, members' skills and capabilities, and foster the professional image without loss of the volunteer ethos. The Society has a great future, John believes, one that is distinct from but collaborative with the shadow CCB.

THE REVEREND DEREK UPCOTT became Vice-Chairman of the Chiltern Society in 1995, Chairman of Chiltern Open Air Museum in 2000, and has represented the Society on the Technical Panel of the shadow Chilterns Conservation Board for most of that time. He is an active Rotarian with a popular nation-wide now, Schools Technology Tournament to his credit. He also gave talks about the Society to the clubs, passing on this job to Cic when he ran out of time, one that Cic has successfully continued. Derek became an ordained Church of England Minister in Secular Employment in 1984, entering the Ministry at the age of 58, and still regularly takes services and helps out at local churches.

"My abiding interest is to help people use their skills and develop new ones, while working with others to achieve mutual objectives. An enabling role in God's creation, one might say."

He has been actively involved in a wide variety of voluntary organisations for more than 60 years, beginning by organising sports activities for his friends during the Second World War, then becoming first a youth leader and then chairman of a post-war area youth committee. Derek had many interests: singing, amateur opera, ballroom dancing, and sports generally, first meeting Cic at the local tennis club. Joining Cic's main interest, he became active in their local Community Association, soon becoming its Chairman and later Chairman of the first local Federation.

On return from five years in the Far East, they settled in Chesham with their young family. In 1969 he was invited to join the Chesham Society, founded in 1957, to take on the Secretary's role. Following the successful Chesham Millennary Festival in 1970, in which he and Cic played large parts, he became Chairman of the Chesham Society, staying for ten years, and Cic took the Secretary's role:

"…during which time our planning team wrote a Town Structure Plan for Chesham, had it accepted by Chiltern District Council, and successfully fought off a proposal to put a large dual carriage-way between Chesham town centre and the Park. This plan was designed to cut off the Old Town and Park area from shops and the commercial centre, unnecessarily destroying many old buildings … Buckinghamshire County Council was required to re-think the scale of its proposals; what is there now is minute compared to what was planned."

Seeking common cause, contact was made between Derek and various members of the Chiltern Society and particularly closely with Peter Mould, then General Secretary of the Society.

"The public consultations into Buckinghamshire's first Structure Plan became the litmus test for the two Societies to agree their mutual interests and share action. In practical terms the Chiltern Society needed the presence of friendly representatives at each hearing, and the Chesham Society was able to provide some of these. The Chiltern Society spoke for those matters concerned with the AONB and its surrounds, and the Chesham Society and similar amenity groups spoke for the more urban areas. This division of interests has pertained ever since, and has worked well over all these years."

Cic was appointed Editor of *Chiltern News* in 1988 and joined the EC, just before Captain Harry Home Cook, RN retired became Chairman.

"He began to move on forming stronger links with its members and constituent bodies. Cic and I attended and supported meetings designed by Harry to form stronger links with members and communities; these were the forerunners of Local Members' Groups. I attracted the eagle eye (and ear) of the good Captain, and was invited to join in his Forward Planning meetings. In 1995 I was elected to the Executive Council, and shortly after that Dr Barry Scott, the successor Chairman to Harry Cook, asked me if I would become Vice Chairman (Internal) alongside Michael Rush who was Vice Chairman (External)"

Derek accepted the invitation, and commenced a partnership with Michael Rush that continued after he was elected Chairman in 1997. Of this association, Derek says:

"Michael Rush began to seek to improve the outside image of the Chiltern Society, strengthening and promoting the organisation's activities, and supporting these by encouraging the continuing recruitment of new members by Edward Newmark. My Vice Chairman's role became both internally and externally oriented to further these aims. This working relationship with Michael has been one of my high points of recent years, bolstered by solid achievements. I cannot say too strongly what a joy it was to work with Michael: we sparked one another off into further creative thinking, much based on our experience as management consultants working in similar fields of industry."

Derek has numerous other duties and assignments on behalf of the Society, which are part of the fun and pleasure of everyday activity. He says of one of them "Life is very exciting." He is on the Board of the Chiltern Woodlands Project, and Ewelme Watercress Beds Management Committee. He attends many meetings inside and outside the Society, including Group Committee meetings, and chairs the Transport Strategy group (TSg) looking at impacts of Government plans on the South-East, and the Chilterns, from housing demands to European requirements, and their impact upon future production and employment requirements and the necessary infrastructure. Finally, he is responsible for overseeing the Volunteer Co-ordinator Programme, now being developed, to ensure its satisfactory outcome for the benefit of all who do conservation and maintenance work in the wider Chilterns.

So, how does Derek see the future? "That's an interesting one," he says.

"As the role of the shadow Chilterns Conservation Board develops, we will still be the largest voluntary body in the Chilterns, able to physically engage with many of the activities envisaged in the AONB plans. Throughout our history we have pressed for this protection of our AONB, so that it may take the lead in those matters where statutory strength is important. There is much to do, and we will have much expected from us, and hoped of us.

"Our primary role has always been one of identifying local needs and acting to secure their satisfaction. Equally we have engaged in cooperative advocacy, both on our own behalf and that of other local amenity societies, large or small. Neither of these roles will change; our continuing presence will be vitally important. All the authorities and agencies involved will need to adjust their thinking to the new situation and accorded responsibilities of the new Board, and work to ensure that an equal partnership of statutory and voluntary bodies is the only constructive and practicable way forward.

"Our immediate tasks are undoubtedly to maintain the excellent working relationships we have had with the shadow Board; to enlarge the area of cooperation and increase our membership that, by definition, will enhance our influence. We will have an important role to play in the future and we must continue to be involved and take initiatives wherever possible.

"Robin Rowland succeeded Michael Rush in October 2002. We had worked together during Michael's time particularly when Robin and his Strategic Development Committee viewed the Society's future, and we agreed some 80 detailed recommendations on the way forward, under two visions: for the Chilterns in the 21st Century, and for the Society in the next ten years. It is stimulating to be at the start of this new perspective; life continues to be full and exciting, under Robin's chairmanship."

Christopher Barry – General Secretary (1968-1971)
My Life in the Chilterns

Christopher might have been a code name for activists in the early days; there were four of us in at the start: Chris Hall, of course, Chris Morris, Chris Wallis and me. All of us were at the founders' meeting, and all of us found ourselves immediately wrapped up in jobs in the embryo society. For my part I had always been interested in old buildings and so I became involved in the group that became Historic Works and Buildings, which I chaired for some time.

The historic tale of how Chris Hall "persuaded" me to take over from him as General Secretary over a couple of pints of Brakspears is perfectly true. I would emphasise that I was not drunk but just flattered that he should have picked on me as his successor. I was conceited enough to let myself believe that I could do the job, my position at the BBC being sufficiently self-regulated to permit me to find time for outside activities.

Although I had agreed to do the job for a maximum three years, I had not reckoned on quite how much work would be involved, especially as the Society was growing fast. I quickly saw that some degree of delegation would be necessary to enable the Society to advance and allow me to cope with the work involved.

Three groups had been formed in the "heady" early days. Historic Works & Buildings, Rights of Way, and Minerals, the catalysts for these being the obvious threats to the environment, the need to stimulate and improve footpath and bridleway coverage of the Chilterns and the need to see some control exercised on the expanding Pitstone Cement works.

By way of spreading the load on the Executive, my term in office was to see the establishment of four more specialist groups: Anti-Litter, Commons, Water Resources and Trees & Woodlands. However, that still left many big areas that were to be primarily the Executive's concern: the Roskill Commission report on the siting of a third London Airport, the establishment of the Chiltern Standing Conference on the AONB and the approaching M40 over the escarpment. Of these the latter was to be closest to my heart (I lived in Stokenchurch) and it had probably been a hidden factor in my agreeing to become more involved as Hon. Sec.

My over-riding memories of this period are centred on the M40 campaign, a forerunner of such causes celebres as Twyford Down and the Newbury by-pass but carried on in a far more gentlemanly fashion – no 'Swampy' living underground or in the trees. Perhaps we were too well-mannered: that was our trouble. Certainly it was letters to *The Times*, well-conducted protest meetings and marches, as well as lobbying in Whitehall that marked our route to ultimate failure, despite the help and services of such distinguished names as landscape architect Sir Geoffrey Jellicoe and naturalist Richard Fitter. Although I have since, perforce, become a frequent traveller on the new motorway, I remain convinced that the Arup-Jellicoe alternative would not only have been less devasting to the escarpment but its very elegance as a practical solution to the much-needed road would have come, like the railway viaducts of the 19th century, to be perceived as a beautiful structure in its own right. I shall never forget when my children were small, tobogganing down the steep snowy slope over the line where the traffic now thunders. And on the day before the road was opened, my wife clambered down its bank with camera to record, both optically and with her ears, the last day of true, peaceful silence on the Chiltern escarpment.

In May 1971, my three years up, I stepped down from the Secretaryship for my admirable friend and colleague (the late) Peter Mould, who relieved my anxiety by actually stepping forward for the post and setting me free to pursue other avenues of activity. I have commented on the small coterie of activists, and I suppose that is how I found myself taking on the post of Membership Secretary for a while, although I remained on the EC for some while longer, rejoined the HW&BG and also later became Chairman of the Woodlands Group, the latter because there was no one else willing to take it on and as a founder member we could not bear to see any group actually go under for lack of a steersman.

During my time with the HWBG, working parties would convene on certain Sundays, as they still do, to clean and scour the chalk surface of Bledlow Cross. On one such occasion, I cleared our presence there with Lord Carrington's land agent and we duly arrived and set to work. Before long a bonfire of torn-up bracken, brambles and weeds was alight with smoke curling into the autumn sky and work was going well. A landrover approached along the bumpy track; a latecomer, perhaps? As it drew closer, it was apparent who was driving: his Lordship. As he drew up I stepped forward, somewhat apprehensive, to explain our presence. Inevitably it was not long before all became clear, just simple misunderstanding and lack of communication. Lord Carrington apologized for interrupting and departed. But I still like to think that if he had been able to concentrate his mind on foreign affairs (he had resigned from the Government at the time of the Argentine invasion of the Falklands, accepting responsibility for failing to foresee it) instead of bothering about us, the Falklands story might have been very different.

That is not the end of this particular story, however. We continued our labours until late in the day and at last, satisfied that the Cross was now as white as we could get it, we extinguished our bonfire and left the scene. Next morning, Monday, I arrived at my BBC office to screaming telephones and my assistant announced that the Buckinghamshire Fire Brigade had been trying desperately to reach me. Coat still on, I grabbed a phone. "Is that Chris Barry?" said an urgent voice. "This is Christopher Barry," I replied, for that is and always has been my professional as well as my correct name. The urgent voice repeated that it belonged to an officer of Bucks Fire Service. My heart sank. Had we failed to extinguish our bonfire and left the escarpment above Bledlow ablaze? "Why? What's up?" I yelled. "It's that demonstration of cutting victims out of smashed cars," he said, "I want to get it settled". Everything became clear. It was not me that he wanted but another BBC director called Chris BErry.'

My active life in the Society continued, somewhat more prosaically – along with my normal BBC career and membership of the Parish Council – until early retirement loomed and with it the question of whether or not we stayed in our beloved Chilterns or moved further from London for a quieter life. I mean that quite literally for by now the M40 was a fait accompli and the noise it generated and threw across Stokenchurch Green and into my home was an ever-present reminder of a battle we had so gallantly lost. But it has a figurative meaning too, for knowing the demands of the beast, I reckoned I needed to leave the Society's area for good or I'd either find or be found more to occupy me for the rest of my life.

I miss the Chilterns and despite the need to escape from the ever-pressing duties undertaken, I have continued to pay my annual subscription for the 18 years since I left, as well as remaining an avid reader of the *News*. We return, my wife and I, fairly often to visit friends or walk in the beechwoods. I don't regret any of the 20-odd years of service I gave the Society, grudging though oftentimes they were, but feel privileged to have been able to help in some small way to maintain the beauty of those woods and of the countryside in which they stand.

Don Brooks – Life Member

There are as many answers to the question, "What made you join the Chiltern Society?" as there are Society members. I can only mention the factors that, in my case, motivated me to join a gathering of like-minded folk represented by the organisation. Probably Christopher Barry provided the trigger prompting my wife, Marjorie, and me to join.

In early summer of 1969 Marjorie and I were going for a walk taking in Pitstone Hill when we met a fellow human who clearly shared our interest in walking. After an exchange of greetings and views common to all lovers of the open-air, we found we also shared his interest in historic buildings. Christopher said something like, "You obviously enjoy walking, why not join the Chiltern Society?" Since we liked his suggestion and found the case for membership was too strong to resist, we joined forthwith, and are now Life Members.

My love of the open-air was probably inherited from my parents who considered a day spent indoors was a day wasted, but what made moving about the Chilterns easier was the purchase of a bike, at the age of 14! (I was now working and could afford such luxuries!) With this mechanical marvel I was able to travel the length and breadth of the Chilterns and become familiar with such treasures as the villages of Hambledon, Ewelme and Fingest.

In 1945 Marjorie and I were married, and for some time after did our travelling by tandem The two years up to around 1950 were absolute bliss since petrol rationing lasted until then. After this time the roads steadily became noisier, more fume-filled, and dangerous. With the arrival of our son this mode of travelling became impractical and we took to "shank's pony" which mode has served us well right up to the present day. However, unfortunately, wheeled traffic is now leaving the roads too, and following us onto the footpaths. Where do we go to next?

In 1998 the tandem frame that had been gathering dust in our garage for many year finally went to two prominent members of the newly formed Chiltern Society cycling group. They offered it a good home, expressing an enthusiasm to restore it to its original resplendent blue livery.

As an electrical engineer, formerly with ICI, and routinely engaged in precise calculation and alignment, I am naturally interested in measurements of all kinds: watts, amps, ohms, volts, and metric measures. This led me to consider issues and matters connected with the measurement of water supply: the world of pH, rainfall, ground-water, stream flow, alleviation of low flow (ALF) and the like. These interests resulted in my being quickly drawn towards the Water Resources Group, under the chairmanship of Bernard Banfield, and Secretary, Vic Wotton. When Bernard retired I became chairman of the now renamed Rivers and Wetlands (Waterlands first) Conservation Group (RWCG), a post in which I served for six years. I represented the Group at meetings of the Executive Council and was, hopefully, able to influence the negotiations resulting in the improvement of the River Misbourne. Later, the experience stood me in good stead when monitoring and water watching the Bulbourne, Gade, Vir, Mimram and Hiz.

Marjorie and I are members of the PhotoGroup whose function is to maintain a photographic record of changes in the Chiltern scene, also to organise a periodic exhibition of Chiltern photographs and last, but not least, to provide material for the Puzzle Picture feature appearing in each issue of *Chiltern News*.

Footnote - As this book goes to print, Don and Marjorie are leaving their beloved Chilterns for Yorkshire to be near their son and family.

Edward Newmark – Membership Secretary 1990 to 2001

In 1989, the Society urgently needed a Membership Secretary; Chairman Harry Cook attended a dinner organised by the Berkhamsted Local Members'group, one of long-standing. There he met Edward and Gerda Newmark, members for many years, and promptly asked Edward to take on this post. Edward describes this request:

"I asked him was there anything I could do to help, when I retired shortly from business life. 'Right', he said in his forthright but very polite manner of a retired naval officer. 'I appoint you membership Secretary and I'll get the Executive Council to agree.' I did not know then that this was the most unpopular job in the Society!"

Edward first visited the Chilterns in the early 30s, travelling with friends to Great Missenden on the Metropolitan Line to walk in the area. In 1936, Gerda came from Vienna with her sister for a holiday, and stayed in Hampstead. She met Edward on one of these walks, and they married shortly after, to live together for more than 60 years. At the outbreak of the war, Edward insisted their small family moved out of London, and so they came to the Chilterns. After the war, a Viennese architect friend designed a modern house for them in Cholesbury, near Chesham, into which they moved in 1952.

Edward shortly after retired from his successful business, when he was just 80, and took up his new position in the Chiltern Society. He described one of his new experiences:

"The EC in 1990 was not a very cohesive body and sometimes Harry had difficulty holding things together. I remember one occasion when a Group representative (who always came to meetings with a vast pile of papers on which to report) being cut short by Harry. Whereupon the man banged his fist on the table and said, '(My Group's business) … is by far and away the most important activity of this Society and…' I interrupted him to say that we all agreed … but would it succeed if there weren't any members?"

The incident, and this lack of cohesiveness in the EC's business activities and procedures undoubtedly were contributing factors to Harry's AUDIT '92 document. A Forward Planning Committee led by Edward presented proposals for procedural reform of the EC, and these were finally approved at the AGM of 1993. A more efficient form of working was established by dividing routine matters from policy development, and placing decision making for the former with a newly created General Purposes Committee.

One of the prime needs in those early days was a Membership Campaign. Edward's account continues:

"In my view Harry Cook was instrumental in enthusing many members and laying the foundations for our future success. It was when Don Millar persuaded British Airways, his employers, to give us £2,500 for environmental work that I jumped at the chance and said that … if I could have part of that money for a membership project I felt sure that, in a year or two, it could be recouped by new membership subscriptions. Harry strongly supported the proposal, and fortunately no-one else had any other project to suggest." (The EC approved the use of £1000 for the purpose.)

"I had realised that lack of publicity was the biggest obstacle to the Society's growth. I had always remembered the story of Pear's Soap: in the early 1900s it had been the biggest advertisers and the best selling soap. One day, the owners said that everyone in the country knew the name Pear's, let us stop spending all this money on advertising. Within a few years Pears was forgotten."

"The best method of reaching the public seemed to be the Royal Mail Door-to-Door mailing scheme. In 20 months we had put a leaflet in every letter box in the Chilterns (except those in the largest towns). The result was that new subscriptions covered the total cost and by the following year, the original investment was more than recouped."

Part of the success was attributable to a newly designed leaflet, designed by a friend of Edward's, who had been design professor also to Peter Hawkes, who undertakes much Society work since he set up his studio in his home town, Chesham.

Membership numbers rose, from around 4000 when Harry Cook became Chairman, to a monthly average for 1992/93 of 5,180 (CN 145, p30). That average was just sustained throughout the next five years, as Edward reported, but he laid the groundwork on which the next advance would be made. A second major recruitment campaign in 1996/97, with more newly designed leaflets, brought more positive results and a momentum that, by mid-2000, resulted in a total membership of 6,513. *Chiltern News* reported the figures and noted "And still climbing". (Issue 157) The much-needed increase in memberships had been achieved.

Gerda Newmark strongly supported her husband's commitment, and was an enthusiastic and willing partner in much of this effort. She had delivered the magazine in their area for many years, and now hosted many meetings at their house, and the first 'get-together'was held there for EC members, new and old, to get to know each other. Gerda treated everyone to traditional Viennese coffee and sweetmeats, and created a welcoming atmosphere to which newcomers could respond, as well as admiring the lovely garden that Edward had created.

In 2001, at the AGM, Edward retired from his role, having seen many changes in the Society, and in the make-up of the EC, during his time in office. By 2001, there were only three of the 1990 group still there,"… and two of those were also retiring". There had been numerous changes in those 11 years, even more following Michael Rush's assumption of the Chairmanship in 1997.

"The changes in the last years under Michael have been far reaching and greater, I think, than the Society has ever seen before. Not only has rising membership led to more funds being available, but Michael has shown that good relations with Government agencies has resulted in grants being obtained for many projects. New computer systems have been installed leading to greater efficiency, more active new members, indeed more of everything.

"But there is always a certain resistance to change. Many members of the EC and elsewhere felt it was more than time to improve our image and change our old-fashioned logo; … it took two years to get general agreement. There is another change that I have wanted since 1991, and from time to time have tentatively suggested it, but without success. That is to change our name. When you mention the Chiltern Society to non-members they immediately ask what is the Society for, what does it do? If we were called the Chiltern Conservation Society everyone would know."

"...my first comment was that I was a then (1991) typical member, but as I only retired from business at age 80, I was not really typical, even then. Nowadays, so many people retire before 60 or 65, and this has led to a much younger group of active members that is making a huge difference to our success. Long may it continue."

Edward's 11-year tenure had achieved the increase in membership so badly needed by the Society for many years, even before he was appointed. He had also helped reform the practices of the EC, and contributed enormously to its deliberations. He is a man with a deep love of the Chilterns, and was still taking his daily 4- or 5-mile walk from his house until very recently. His interest also covers the development of the area as a place where people have lived and worked for centuries. In the magazine of December 2000, he describes how, in 1832 just prior to the Poor Law Reform and the year of the great Parliamentary Reform Bill, his parish of Cholesbury had become bankrupt. He describes the actions of the then Vicar, the Reverend Henry Jeston to care for his parishioners and return the parish to solvency; Edward was a modern day Jeston when he came to work for the Society to make it a successful and usefully constructive organisation caring for the Chilterns.

Gerda sadly died in late 2002, and Edward has left his home for so many years to live in Berkhamsted.

PIONEERS AND FOUNDERS

Bernard Banfield – a great Chiltern conservationist Bernard Banfield was one of the founder members of the Chiltern Society who attended that meeting on 8 May 1965 at the High Wycombe Guildhall, and one of its most persistently active and enthusiastic members until his death, aged 95, in 2001.

On that first occasion he raised the issue of chalk quarrying and cement manufacture at Pitstone as matters of concern. It was to remain part of the Planning Team's portfolio for the next 34 years. He pursued this untiringly, on one occasion taking the case to Parliament, famously chaining his bicycle to the railings of the House of Commons. When the Cement Liaison Committee was convened by Bucks County Council, Bernard represented the Chiltern Society thereon for many years, appearing at Public Inquiries into continuing developments. At the Inquiry into proposals for a refuse tip in Quarry 2, (1994) then aged 88, he supported Geoffrey Legge and other Society witnesses on almost every one of the 38 days, often with Elsie, his wife.

Among his many interests was water and he was an indefatigable supporter of the Water Resources Group, eventually becoming its Chairman. He was particularly interested in plans for re-opening the Wendover Arm of the Grand Union Canal and served on the local committee formed to promote this. He was also a keen ally of Vic Wotton when Vic embarked on his crusade to save the flow and quality of the River Misbourne. This action in turn led to a realisation by Government that chalk streams are invaluable to the environment and their water had to be conserved by limiting extraction from them.

His encyclopaedic knowledge of, and interest in local matters has been of immense help to those in the Chiltern Society who are active in the Ivinghoe and Pitstone area. He and Elsie were founder members of the Beacon Villages Association, many of whose Parish Councillors he helped to persuade to become members of the Chiltern Society. His wider interests in Chiltern issues and his great enthusiasm for pursuing these sometimes brought him into conflict with less committed authorities and individuals. He was a great contributor to *Chiltern News*, sometimes in verse, and rarely without his sense of humour showing through.

Bernard was a professional radio engineer, and maintained a lasting interest in electrical and radio engineering; he was responsible for installing radios in airships being built at Cardington in the early 1930s. He was also then a deeply committed youth leader, and supporter of the Youth Hostels Association. In Shelley Savage's small book: *Water from Wendover; the story of the Wendover Arm Canal*, publiished in 2002, there is a short piece, written by Bernard, about his connection with a London Youth Club.

"Refugees on the Arm

"Before the 1939 War, there was a solidly built double canal-side house, with large, deep cellars, between Drayton Beauchamp and Little Tring, called The White Houses, date c.1820. They were occupied by two families of maintenance canal folk who controlled the adjacent submarine sluice that can divert the eastward flowing Arm water away from the mainline canal summit at Bulbourne, into a deep adit feeding the Wilstone Reservoirs.

"In November 1938 the houses, which had wonderful mature gardens, choice fruit trees (including the luscious golden gage, never seen nowadays) and a 100ft well, were vacant.

"A London Youth Club, with which my wife and I were closely associated, rented the double house, knocked it into one, cleaned out the well (dozens of lost buckets and several bike frames recovered), and took in refugees from Nazi Germany and Austria, mostly Jewish. This was with generous financial help from the Quakers.

"My wife ran the venture as a voluntary warden. Many of the refugees were broken psychologically, and racked by anxiety for relations still within Hitler's reach.

"During the blitz, Londoners came down each night to get some sleep and were put up in every nook and cranny of the house. … In 1942 the landmine that parachuted down in Aylesbury, six miles away, blew open doors and windows in the refugee building.

"After the war, the houses fell vacant again. Regrettably the then canal authority levelled the buildings and garden and filled in the well, on the poor pretext that there was no right-of-way to this very desirable country cottage; end of epoch. Bernard Banfield, 14 Feb 1990."

Geoffrey Legge, Planning Co-ordinator of the Chiltern Society joined with Bernard on many of the public representations of the Pitstone quarry case. He came to know him well.

Writing in *Chiltern News* in March 2001, Geoffrey says:

> "I think it is fair to say that there has not been one Society Group in which he has not taken some part or interest - he even invented and promoted a (single) pedal bike when one of his legs seized up. Bernard never missed an AGM until after he was 90. When I visited him in a nursing home two weeks before he died, he asked me to bring him up to date by taking him through the Society's Annual Report."

Bernard's determination to succeed stood him in good stead, and he was the embodiment of natural courtesy. In memory of Bernard, his long residence in Ivinghoe, and his involvement in many local groups, clubs and societies concerned with the quality of Pitstone and Ivinghoe life, the Wendover Arm Trust, the Chiltern Society and many others contributed towards a memorial seat to be installed on Ivinghoe village green, where he had lived. Bernard will be remembered by many people, members of the Society and others alike, as one of the great men who cared passionately for the Chilterns landscape in which he lived..

Archie Campbell - General Secretary (1975-1981)

Written by Christopher Morris, Vice-President and founder member, who remembers a great General Secretary with whom he worked as Chairman. Christopher is still active in the Society as a member of the Planning Steering Group; he lives in Hertfordshire.

Archie Campbell took over as the fourth General Secretary of the Society in 1975, following an interregnum caused by Peter Mould's work taking him overseas and preventing his continuing in the post. Those at the centre of the Society heaved a sigh of relief when Archie arrived and brought to an end the uncertainty about the future direction of the organisation. He had most excellent credentials for the job having been brought up in the Chilterns, lived there on and off for many years and developed a great love for them. He was educated at Berkhamsted School, like the founder of the Society, Chris Hall, and at Hertford College, Oxford. He qualified as a Barrister-at-Law and served in the Colonial Office in the Gold Coast, Washington and Malta and finally achieved high office in the Ministry of Defence. During his colonial service he was made a Companion of the Order of St.Michael and St.George (CMG).

In Archie's day, as in that of his predecessors, Peter Mould, Chris Barry and Chris Hall, the General Secretary was essentially the Society's chief executive, and he soon got a grip on the Society's affairs. His administrative skills were invaluable. He quite rightly proceeded on the basis that the General Secretary's role was not to do everything himself but to know what was going on, to understand what had to be done and to try to ensure that it was and to act as a catalyst for new activities. One of his major administrative successes was, with Kitty Bird, to organise the distribution of *Chiltern News* by an army of volunteers with a consequent dramatic improvement in the Society`s finances.

It would be very wrong however, to suggest that Archie's main contribution was to administration. He immersed himself in the planning and strategic problems of the Chilterns and played a co-ordinating role in the formulation and presentation of the Society`s views on countryside policies. There were, for example, starting in 1976, the Sandford Report on National Parks, papers from the Department of the Environment`s Countryside Review Committee, especially *The Countryside Problems and Policies*, and a review by Himsworth commissioned by the Countryside Commission, on what AONB designation of an area had achieved. In connection with the latter the Countryside Review Committee had put forward proposals for radical changes to the concept of National Parks and the AONBs. The Chiltern Society responded to all of these and, although Peter Mould and Peter Cuming provided a large part of the necessary effort, Archie took the lead in the submission of its comments on the Countryside Review Committee's proposals and in all the input to the AONB review. He also represented the Society on the Chiltern Standing Conference, the one body that was supposed to look after the AONB as a whole and which the Society had sought to keep alive, if only by producing well thought out papers on crucial subjects which the Conference could not avoid discussing. At the time this was only partially successful but the effort was not wasted. Later the Conference was revitalised, and with its transformation into the 'shadow' Chilterns Conservation Board of today, has become a significant force in the guarding of the Chilterns' AONB.

In 1979 it was not found possible to get someone to take on the Editorship of *Chiltern News*. Archie took over this position as well – "temporarily". He continued as Editor for the next 18 months, although some issues were produced by others during this period to give him a break. He set up an editorial board to spread the load but the management remained with him. He also contributed many articles and wrote with clarity of style on complicated issues. The Society had reason to be proud of the *News*, its one means of communication with the great majority of its members, and, although its high standards had been set by his predecessors, Archie continued the tradition most ably.

Another subject in which he took a particular interest was the problem of aircraft noise, which afflicts the Chilterns from both Heathrow and Luton. He became expert in the operations of London Air Traffic Control, maintained contact with other interested bodies such as Luton and District Association for the Control of Aircraft Noise (LADACAN) and made sure that the Society`s voice was well and truly heard.

In 1980 he was asked to go to Rhodesia as a member of the British team observing the first post independence elections. Later that year my heart sank when he told me that he would not be standing again as General Secretary at the AGM in October; I knew that there would be great difficulty in finding a successor and so it proved. In fact Archie continued in the post until 1981 to help in the search that was not entirely successful. Until Christopher Tatham took over in 1987 it was not possible to find someone who could devote the time required for more than a year or two. As a consequence the Chairmen who followed me had to play a more executive role in the running of the Society and this continues to the present day

Throughout his Secretaryship, Archie Campbell was strongly supported by Peggy, his wife. She had to put up with all the demands on his time and to entertain at their home the frequent meetings of the News' editorial board and other Society committees. This she did with good grace; it was partly her poor health that made Archie resign from the Secretaryship. He did however undertake to write, in 1982, the second volume of the Society`s history *Seventy Five – Eighty One*.

It is not to be supposed that Archie was a 'Sir Humphrey' type. He had a great sense of humour, was a keen gardener, enjoyed walking, climbing, fishing, and in his younger days was a good cricketer. He was capped for the Buckinghamshire Minor Counties team. He proved an excellent representative for the Chiltern Society on the Southern Council for Sport and Recreation. More surprisingly, perhaps, he was an excellent baker of bread and maker of jam,much enjoyed by visitors. He died on 2 May 1994, sorely missed by those who knew him – one of the Chiltern Society greats.

Anthony Emery – A dedicated Planning Adviser

Tony, who sharpened the attention to planning within the Chiltern Society, first joined it in 1975. Like many other members he belonged to the Rights of Way Group, enjoying the countryside through walking with congenial companions.

Affectionately known as "Doc" for most of his 39 years with, first British Aluminium and then their successors, Alcan, Dr Tony Emery retired from full-time employment at the Company's research base in Chalfont Park, in 1988, aged 65. He continued there as a part-time consultant for a further eight years.

He was an industrial chemist, a specialist and dedicated research worker. He had a reputation for high integrity, meticulousness to a fine degree in the experiments, tenacity in the pursuit of truth and accuracy, and an almost fastidious precision in reporting the results he achieved. His knowledge and expertise were greatly respected by his employers; he had numerous patents to his credit.

These qualities he brought to the role of Planning Adviser, in 1991; the job was then linked to the post of Vice-Chairman. Following the introduction of the Forward Planning Committee's recommendations in 1994, he relinquished the latter appointment, continuing for a further two years and several months as Planning Adviser. He died in January 1997, aged 74.

Tony Emery chaired the Rights of Way Group from 1975 to 1983. John Coombe (ROWG Chairman from 1996) remembers him well, as a deeply committed predecessor. Peter Cleasby, later Roads and Transport Adviser and a member of the planning team, became ROWG Secretary for three years during Tony Emery's chairmanship. He has written:

"Tony was one of the first people I met on joining the Society ... this was not surprising, given the breadth of his interests. His last years with us were, most visibly, as Planning Adviser, a demanding job, possibly the most demanding job in the Society, and one where it is impossible to please everybody. Tony steered all of us through some difficult issues and all on that planning team were grateful for his advice and his knowledge."

Peter Cleasby added:

"I suspect his true passion was for our rights of way. ... This led to many lively, and sometimes protracted, Committee discussions."

Peter pays tribute to Tony's capacity to focus on the issues and bring problems to a resolution;

"The excellent state of the rights of way network in the Chilterns is due in no small measure to Tony's sustained efforts."

Tony Emery was a man with many capabilities and skill endowments. His parents gave him the love of music and sport that went with him throughout life. He learned and developed his piano skills by playing in Sunday School and church; he was a firm Christian, a member first of the Congregational Church and then the United Reform Church when that was established in 1972, uniting the Presbytarian Church of England and the Congregationalists.

He loved and played top-level table tennis until late in life. He is reported to have: " ... bought a new bat to improve his topspin" in his last year of life. He enjoyed cricket, listening to music and entertaining others with performances and gramophone recitals. Almost anticipating his death, he planned so that others might take over the commitments he had taken on when fully fit.

With his qualities of honesty, integrity, fastidiousness, precision in the search for truth, and keenness of mind second to none, Cic Upcott, Editor of *Chiltern News* wrote, " That is how we in this Society remember him."

Tony Emery was Chairman of the Rights of Way Group (1975-83) Planning Adviser to the Chiltern Society (1991-97). Compiled from his obituary in Chiltern News (No.144, June 1997), the Society's Annual Meeting reports and general records.

Don Gresswell – a great Chilterns Conservationist

Don Gresswell first arrived in the area in 1966, owner of an educational furnishing company in Enfield, into which he put many hours work. Despite this, he also put in far more creative work for conservation than any other member of his time – or even two or three of them together, according to Archie Campbell's account!

He persuaded and cajoled, by personal appeal, and inspired by personal example countless others to do even more than they thought they could, and certainly more than they intended. The response to his leadership was the more ready in that Don, with over twice the years of many of his co-workers, out-enthused, out-planned and out-worked even the best of them: character of this calibre is rare, and effort on this scale is invaluable. No problem was too small: it is not so well-known that Don took one example of litter, the tin can, and through thoughtful and gentle persuasion, finally persuaded the producers to use aluminium in their products, resulting in the recyclable item we know today.

He was the Society's right arm. In addition to the material improvement to the environment which his work achieved, there was the appreciation of the Society's name in national and international circles.

The award of a Silver Jubilee Medal in 1977 and the MBE in 1983, both for his work in conservation, perhaps crowned earlier awards such as the one for his work with the Keep Britain Tidy Group (Queen Mother's Birthday Honours Award, 1983); the George Mitchell prize for outstanding leadership for young working parties in the Chilterns (1981); the recognition of the Appalachian Mountain Club, USA; the Vice-Presidency of the British Trust for Conservation Volunteers, and many other honours and offices.

It is largely due to Don that the work of the Society in footpath preservation, waymarking, scrub clearance and litter control has become known, not only in America, but also in France, Japan and New Zealand. The Chiltern Society is in the front rank of conservation societies in the UK and Don Gresswell did more than anyone else to put it there.

The Chiltern Society's several offices held by Don run from his leadership of the Rights of Way Group (Chairman then Hon. Secretary from 1966-1973,) during which years the network of 2,500 miles was completed, and earning a Countryside Award in 1970; the leadership of the Litter Group from 1973 to 1977; then of the Conservation Group until 1979; the foundation of the Chiltern Conservation Volunteers (ConsVols) and the work of scrub clearance on the downlands and on overgrown village ponds.

Don became a member of the Executive Council and was elected Vice President in 1981.

The direction of his energies was always practical; he was not a great committee man but if something needed doing like the planning and installation of stiles Don was ready. The creation, transport by the RAF, and erection of a cairn of Sarsen stones at 269.5m (876ft) on the highest point of the Chilterns is an example of his imagination. This was a contribution to the Queen's Silver Jubilee celebrations. Archie Campbell remarked: "The cairn marked (in an unobtrusive way of course) a very high point in his organisational genius." (Vol.II.p17)

The Society was impoverished by his death, in a literal sense. It is not generally known - because he was a modest man - how much money he gave. The Open Air Museum, the Woodland Project, the publication of the Society's booklets, the cost of the stiles, all were paid for or helped. It is not too much to say that if a worthwhile project needed money, Don would see that it did not fail for lack of it. He was as generous with his support as he was with his time and energy.

In any practical venture Don was your man – not only because one could rely on personal involvement, but also one knew that he would inspire others to give their support. Nick Moon, deviser of the Chiltern Way and author of numerous guides to Chiltern footpaths, acknowledges Don Gresswell's influence upon youthful enthusiasm and lifelong enjoyment of the Chilterns. Christopher Wallis told the author that he, and his wife, Barbara, joined the Society as the result of Don's inspiration. Don Millar, who succeeded Don Gresswell as leader of the Conservation Volunteers learned from, and was inspired by, his namesake.

Dedication to a cause on the scale that Don showed over 20 years would not have been possible had not his wife, Eileen, fully supported him in his work. One had only to see the size of Don's collection of books, papers, and indices, photographs, telephone references and so on, to imagine the distraction that his many activities must have caused in peaceful domesticity. But Eileen never allowed this to get between Don and the Society, and it is fitting that the Society should pay its tribute to the part she played in enabling him to succeed.

Elsie and Bernard Banfield, founder members of the Chiltern Society, knew Don before the Second World War. On his death in 1986, Bernard wrote:

"We have known Don since 1931; even then he was active in voluntary service. Directing with two others in their spare time a successful, non-profit making limited company, International Youth Tours based on the Youth House in London.

"This Company sent thousands inexpensively abroad on tramping or fixed centre holidays in areas of outstanding beauty, bringing the participants into close touch with other Europeans, and attempting to reduce the national tensions building up all over the Continent during the 1930s."

Don Gresswell was one of the Chiltern Society's great leaders and exemplars. He inspired and believed in its ultimate success. In many respects the organisation owes its present strength to his energy, enthusiasm, insight and capacity to achieve the almost impossible.

[See also report of this event in Part 2 (also Vol II) of the main text. Grid reference to the Silver Jubilee Cairn: OS Pathfinder 1094. GR 891091. CS Map. 18. Close to Cedars Car Park: GR 889092 - Source of Reference: CS Map but not shown on OS Maps.]

Compiled from writings and notes by Bernard Banfield, Archie Campbell, Charles Mills, Nick Moon, Guy Patterson, and Chiltern News reports, and Howard Gilbert's conversations with members of the Chiltern Society who still remember Don with affection. May 2003. HG.

Don Millar – a dedicated conservationist and resourceful activist.

Don was born in 1939 and brought up in Perth, Scotland, and came South after the Second World War. After a trip to Canada and a sojourn in their Navy, he returned to Britain opting for service in the RAF. Don was posted to the Far East serving in the liaison team that shepherded VIPs on a variety of critical political missions. A serious accident forced his return home to the UK, and acceptance of an honourable discharge from the Service.

After leaving the RAF he met Diana, married, and came to live in Holmer Green with their young daughters. Two years later he met Don Gresswell in their local pond clearance meet, and was, as many of his contemporaries had been, influenced to positive involvement in conservation and began working with the Chiltern Society's Conservation Volunteers Bureau, its original title.

After that seminal meeting Don Millar gradually developed a deep and profound interest in the quality of the countryside in which he lived. This was later to extend to the boundaries of the AONB and the Society in South Oxfordshire, and in the northern reaches in Bedfordshire. The Ewelme Watercress Beds received his Group's attention and support; the north Chilterns felt his guiding hand on conservation issues. In central Chilterns, the Open Air Museum found him providing poultry to stock the Victorian Farm, and the Executive Council's membership drive, spearheaded by Edward Newmark, gained immensely from his advocacy to his employers, British Airways and their grant to fund environmental work.

Don Millar took over the work of organising countryside clearance groups following Don Gresswell's death in 1986. He inherited one main unit that, as the workload expanded, was divided into three separate operating groups. Later, responding to the desire of some retired volunteers to work mid-week, he encouraged the formation of the Mid-Week group, providing them with support and assistance. By the mid-Nineties there were four Conservation Volunteer groups: North, Central and South Chilterns, and the Mid-Week Volunteers group; each had their own leader/co-ordinator, respectively: Ron Horne, Julie Wilson, Christine Breden, Beryl Hunt, with Ray Wainwright, and other mid-week volunteers taking it in turns to organise the mid-week operation, but still dependent on Don to obtain the work.

Don's immense commitment to Chiltern Society conservation is clear from two communications to Cic Upcott during the three weeks or so before he died, hastened by his and Di's intention to take a world tour. An e-mail of 16 December 2001 and a report in early January 2002 from Don gave the current group structure, the way things were changing and the prospect of a professional Countryside Officer to organise the work schedule and recruit volunteers.

"The appointment to this position is very exciting for me," he wrote. "I have worked hard over many months, with others in the Society, to prove the need for this post."

In the same communication he announced his own retirement from British Airways, and his plans for roughly doubling the scale of the ConsVols operation over the

"next few years. The intent is to assist the new Trees, Hedgerows and Woodland Group and The Chiltern Woodlands Project under John Morris to tackle new areas of possible volunteer work. I also hope that we can do some survey work for the Historic Works & Buildings Group, and also for the Rivers and Wetlands Group. The intent is to have a person in post who can also train our volunteers in country crafts and related areas, so that we can, for instance, do a Hedgerow Survey."

Don Millar made sure that when a professional job needed doing, the necessary apparatus and support were on hand. In the email he outlines the Conservation Volunteers' progress in skill, capacity, and scale of operations over a ten-year span.

"We started with light hand tools in 1992. (Now) by 2001 we have five chain saw operators fully trained with three chain saws. There are six scrub cutters and one strimmer. All operators of this equipment receive training as do also the users of our five hedge trimmers. (We have) one cycle scythe mower and a small chipper. We, in this year, have every hand-tool we need for every type of job we are asked to tackle.

"Week-end groups are now two main Groups with Don Millar in the middle of the Chilterns and Beryl Hunt in the South who also looks after the Ewelme Watercress Beds.

"We intend, in 2002, to expand further, with the aid of a countryside officer. We started working with Bucks County Council in 1994 on the Parish Partnership Project that, for the first time, allowed us to obtain payments for some of our work on footpaths and bridleways. In 2002 we hope to expand to Bedfordshire and Hertfordshire (this work). I cannot think of any other special events"

For Don Millar, ConsVols work was serious, important, professional and dedicated to conserving the countryside. That he enjoyed it enormously is clear from the tribute in *Chiltern News* for March 2001 and the photographs that surround it.

"He never seemed to stop, talking, laughing, working, falling asleep, snoring (even in committee meetings) ..."

He also believed in feasting after a job well done. A phase of work on the Misbourne had been successfully completed, and was celebrated in style on 21 May 1988, at the Royal Oak, near Great Missenden. In a jointly organised occasion with Ken Poyton from Marlow, the Conservation Volunteers welcomed all Society members to a Bonfire and Barbecue. The fire was needed to warm the late spring air, and a tent was provided in case of inclement weather; the food was cooked on a large barbeque in the Royal Oak grounds. Music for a barn dance was provided by the Marlow Group, the Shop was in attendance and there was a display of Society activities.

The event was timed "from 6pm until 11pm. There will be a guided tour of this beautiful private stretch of the River Misbourne. Ancient wooded area, old watercress beds and BBONT nature reserve."

Don Millar died suddenly, on 18 January 2002 and was deeply mourned by many who knew him. The following Minute records of his attendance at his first Executive Council meeting on 1 November 1986:

"The Chairman introduced Don Millar who had stepped into Don Gresswell's shoes. Don Millar said he was finding out that Don Gresswell had been a "giant in the conservation field."

Undoubtedly, one giant was succeeded by another. Don Millar devoted 15 years of his life, and an immensity of his leisure time to caring for the Chiltern Hills. He was one of the Society's great conservationists.

Compiled from reports produced in Chiltern News and other Chiltern Society documents and records between 1981 and 2001. HG

Where he most loved to be - up to his knees in muddy water.

THE CHILTERN STORY ENDS, THE CHILTERN STORY BEGINS

In the June 2003 issue of *Chiltern News*, Robin Rowland, Chairman of the Chiltern Society, wrote

" ...how lucky we are to live in the Chilterns and how important it is to keep it as an attractive and special area in which people can live and work. It has always been a place for visitors to enjoy."

He went on to say that, with the pressures exerted by contemporary life and work in the South East, the Chiltern Society is "as relevant as we ever were" and must continue to be specially vigilant for our heritage. Perhaps also it is not without significance that the CPRE has recently changed and shortened its name to become the Campaign to Protect Rural England. How best to conserve? How best to protect? How best to share? How best to enjoy? How to secure and sustain that delicate balance between city, growing urbanisation, residential countryside, rural South East England? This history is not the place to answer those questions; it is the moment, as the Society moves into a new phase of its life, to present them as continuing issues.

No one would argue today that the Chilterns should not change. Whilst writing this history I became much aware that the Chilterns had changed considerably during the 36 years from the Society's foundation. And the Society too, has changed, become larger, more mature, better informed and having a widening influence upon life and work in the AONB. Change is the stuff of history. It is what history is about; without change and transition there would be nothing to record beyond what is. My successor in 30 or so years' time will record much change from where the Society is today.

One of my reference books was William Cobbett's *Rural Rides*, first published in 1830 but often referring to a time ten or twenty or more years earlier. The author, a gentleman radical, rode through part of the Chilterns seven years after the defeat of Napoleon at Waterloo in 1815. This was a time when many of the pressures which we experience today were germinating or in embryo. In politics the slow dawn of a popular franchise was coming closer. In agriculture the enclosure movement was reaching its peak, with dramatic effect upon the English landscape. The Parliamentary will to commute tithes (already often locally practiced) was near at hand. Change was everywhere present. The price of bread and the continuation of the Corn Laws were politically and economically matters of argument and debate. In town and in the countryside there was evidence of the increasing use of machines displacing traditional craft skills, cultivation practice on the land and in the workshops. There were instances of rural unrest, discontented farm workers, riots, rick-burning and opposition to the introduction of farm machinery.

Cobbett was wary of too much change and his Chiltern notes suggest something close to an idyllic rural life. In this passage he seems to be arguing two things: all's well with rural England and its people and, for the town dwellers, why do they need the vulgarity of pleasure grounds, then much in vogue, when there is such beautiful, idyllic countryside in which to enjoy life and recreation. He offers an Arcadian view of a time which history shows was undoubtedly changing at a quickening pace.

Starting from Kensington in the early morning he describes what he sees in a day. Even then there were examples of ' daily commuters' to the City from the countryside, so nothing strange in him travelling the other way when daylight was at its longest hour. Five days earlier he had travelled to St Albans via Stanmore and Watford.

"Kensington, 24 June 1822
Set out at four this morning for Redbourn, and then turned off Westward to go to High Wycombe through Hempstead and Chesham. The wheat is good all the way. The custom is in this part of Hertfordshire, (and I am told continues all the way into Bedfordshire) to leave a border round the ploughed part of the fields to bear grass, and to make hay from, so that, the grass being now made into hay, every cornfield has a closely mown grass walk about ten foot wide all round it, between the corn and the hedge. This is most beautiful! The hedges are now full of shepherd's rose, honeysuckles, and all sorts of wild flowers; so that you are on a grass walk with this most beautiful of flower gardens and shrubberies on your hand and with the corn on the other hand. And thus you go from field to field (on foot or horseback) the sort of corn, the sort of underwood and timber, the shape and size of the fields, the height of the hedgerows, the height of the trees, all continually varying. Talk of pleasure grounds indeed!"

These pleasure grounds were probably Vauxhall Gardens and the North London imitators at Hampstead, Marylebone, Sadlers Wells, Islington and elsewhere. Begun in the previous century as places of high society entertainment, they had changed to cater for more populist tastes. By 1822 they had a reputation for bawdiness and vulgarity; this is what Cobbett's stricture was about. He continues:

"All along the country that I have come the labourer's dwellings are good. They are made of what they call brick-nog (that is to say, a frame of wood, and a single brick thick, filling up the vacancies between the timbers). They are generally covered with tile. Not pretty by any means; but they are good; and you see here, as in Kent, Surrey, Sussex and Hampshire, and indeed almost every part of England, that most interesting of all objects, that which is such an honour to England, and that which distinguishes it from all the rest of the world, namely, those neatly kept and productive little gardens round the labourer's houses, which are seldom ornamented with more or less of flowers. We have only to look to know what sort of people these English labourers are: these gardens are the answer to the Malthuses and Scarletts.

Here Cobbett makes reference to the then current theory, propounded by Thomas Malthus in 1798 that the population developing at its contemporary rate, unchecked, was increasing by geometrical progression, but the means of subsistence only did so arithmetically. Malthus concluded that the outcome would be mass starvation. He condemned the Poor Laws of the time arguing that they encouraged large families, and also advocated later marriage amongst labourers.

It is useful to contrast Cobbett's singular view of the Chilterns with that of Leslie W Hepple and Alison M Doggett in their chapter about the 19th century Chilterns. They describe a changing countryside as early as 1800, which was to reflect, throughout the century, the shifting balance between the outward spread of urban landscape and the sustainment of rural quality, ultimately assisted by Green Belt delineation.

Three extracts from their writing serve to illustrate the movements and forces driving change. These are the opening lines of their chapter:

"If we could have stood on the top of Coombe Hill near Wendover around the year 1800, we would have seen a landscape in transformation. The great canal from London to Birmingham had just been constructed across Tring summit, a branch to Wendover was being built, and the land would have seemed torn and scarred. In the Vale the process of enclosure by Parliamentary Acts was well under way, replacing the open fields with a new planned landscape of enclosed and hedged fields."

Enclosure in the Hills had been earlier, beginning in some instances during Tudor times, in the 16th century. The change came much earlier than in the Vale, often because only one owner was involved and unlikely to be challenged. The earliest enclosures were connected with sheep farming. Those later in the Vale and elsewhere were for both animal husbandry and crops. Commons and heaths were often at risk during the later changes.

"The piecemeal enclosure within the Hills after 1550 had not destroyed the major heaths and commons. They had been nibbled at and eroded in places, mostly small-scale but ranging up to 300 acres taken from Berkhamsted Frith in 1616. Late 18th century maps, like Davis' of Oxfordshire, demonstrate the sharp contrast of open Vale and enclosed Chiltern, but they also show large areas of common surviving within the Hills. They included Wycombe and Holmer Green, Naphill Common, Prestwood Common, Stokenchurch and Chequers Common. In the Hertfordshire Chilterns there were commons at Berkhamsted, Wigginton and Cholesbury; in Oxfordshire there were heaths at Goring, Checkendon, Chazey, and Ipsden, and such lists could be extended."

Cottage craft industries of straw plaiting and lacemaking were widely spread in the small villages and communities. Bedfordshire pillow lace was much sought after, and silk was manufactured at Tring. High farming prosperity in the 1850s and 60s was followed after 1875 by a depression that continued almost unabated into the 1940s and affected most of the rural crafts and cottage industries too.

"The farming depression was part of a wider rural decline with crafts like lace, straw and wood-bodging also declining. Rural incomes fell, there was little investment, and people were migrating from the land. Many Chiltern parishes saw their population fall in these years. But population growth in the commuter towns and settlements along the railway lines offset much of the rural losses in the Chilterns themselves, and the region suffered nothing like the declines experienced in North Buckinghamshire. The Chilterns' accessibility to London continued to make them attractive as a location for a country home for the wealthy, like the London solicitor Sir Frank Crisp who built Friar Park outside Henley in 1889/90. The biggest Impact of 'outside money' was felt at Tring and Aston Clinton, where the Rothschild family had a whole network of country houses They spent a lot of money in these depression years rebuilding farmhouses and entire villages in the distinctive Rothschild gothic-cum-Swiss style, with tall, twisting chimneys."

The end of the century does indeed mark an important transition for the Chilterns. The traditional rural scene was in decay, setting in train changes in the landscape of woods and downs that only had their full impact over many decades. At the same time the area was becoming a dormitory region for London, a role that was to increase dramatically after the turn of the century. It was a new balance that had to be achieved between town and country."

The Chiltern Society, and today's Chiltern residents are the inheritors of the changes described by Hepple and Doggett. The balance between town and country continued to change throughout the 20th century. It can be argued that the designation of the AONB in 1966 was an acknowledgement of a national problem then threatening an imbalance that had to be redressed. Recent changes, the hoped for confirmation of the 'shadow' Chilterns Conservation Board and the momentum towards Regional planning regulation may also be seen in that light although the latter lacks proof, appears geographically impossible and (as yet in 2003) has no democratic validation. This history of the Chiltern Society ends at a point where another chapter is about to begin.

The Society has a new charitable status and direction; it is developing a strong relationship with the shadow Chilterns Conservation Board that it has done much in the past to foster and secure. The project achievements at Lacey Green, in the Chiltern woodlands, at the Chiltern Open Air Museum and the Ewelme Watercress Beds, witness to its capacity and capability in environmental matters. Society membership is growing, and with members making new and different demands, seeking new projects and purposes, this may be as important and acute a moment of change as that on 8 May, 1965 when 100 supporters of a meeting convened by Christopher Hall and the late Ted Castle decided to form the Chiltern Society. Is this moment the end <u>and</u> the beginning?

ABOVE *Nothing's changed – footpath workers treading down a lost path over a ploughed field at Beacon Hill, in early days.*

ABOVE *Stiles come in named varieties – this is the type known as Dreadnought, but Don Gresswell has added a bottom step and top rail to make it easier.*

ABOVE *Sir Bernard Miles and Christopher Wallis at the Opening of Lacey Green Windmill*

ABOVE *Going, going, nearly gone! The last Pitstone chimney coming down.*

ABOVE *January 1986 – the dried bed of the Misbourne*
RIGHT *Rover scouts working at Berkhamsted restoring steps*

ABOVE *The great clean up of East Wood, Stokenchurch, one of the very early projects of the Anti-Litter Group*

Chris Hall

Peter Mould

Charles Mills

Christopher Morris

Nick Moon

Barry Scott

Michael Rush

Sir John Johnson

Sir Leonard Figg

BIBLIOGRAPHY

Beckett I F W	*Buckinghamshire*, 1995
Birch C (FRSA)	*Chiltern Thames in Camera*, 1980
Cannon J (Ed)	*The Oxford Companion to British History*, 1997
Clarke P, Jackson B,	
Mercer D, (Eds)	*The Sunday Times Book of the Country*, 1986
Cobbett Wm	*Rural Rides*, 1984 (from original in 1885)
Greeves L Trinick M	*The National Trust Guide* (4th edition),1989
Cull, Elizabeth	*Portrait of the Chilterns*,1982
Hastie S & Spain D	*A Hertfordshire Valley*, 1996
Hepple L W &	
Doggett A M	*The Chilterns* (2nd edition), 1994
Hoskins W G	*Local History in England*, 1959
Hyde T, Poyton K,	
Upcott C, (et al)	*Treasures of the Chilterns*, 1999
Ingram R	*The Ridgeway, Europe's Oldest Road*, 1988
Johnson P (Ed)	*20th Century Britain*, 1994
Lloyd T O	*English History 1906-1992*, (4th edition), 1993
Legh J M	*The Story of Ewelme Watercress*, 1999
Massingham H J	*Chiltern Country* (2nd edition), 1943
Moon N	*The Chiltern Way*, 2000
Morris J K	*History of the Chiltern Woodlands*, 1999
Adams R (et al)	*AA Book of British Villages*
Richardson B (Ed)	*The Hertfordshire Way*, 1998
Savage S	*Water from Wendover*, 2002
Stidworthy, J (et al)	*Bottom Wood*, 1994
Thomas, S & P	*On Your Bike – The Chilterns*, 2001
Wotton V H	*Misbourne Miscellany*, 1990
	To Rescue a River, 1987

References have also been made in the text to volumes of the Chiltern Society histories, to papers from the appropriate organisation as indicated, and to *Chiltern News* magazine, various issues.

ABBREVIATIONS

AGM	Annual General Meeting
ALFs	Alleviation of Low Flows (Chiltern Chalk Streams)
AONB	Area of Outstanding Natural Beauty
BBC	British Broadcasting Corporation
BBONT	Berkshire, Buckinghamshire and Oxfordshire Naturalists Trust
BBOWT	Berkshire, Buckinghamshire and Oxfordshire Wildlife Trust
CASC	Chiltern Area Survey Commission
CC (and **CA**)	Countryside Commission (from 1999, Countryside Agency)
CCCV	Central Chilterns Conservation Volunteers
CCV	Chiltern Conservation Volunteers
CN	Chiltern News
COAM	Chiltern Open Air Museum,
CPRE	Council for the Preservation (Protection) of Rural England (from 2003 the Campaign to Protect Rural England)
ConsVols	acronym for CCV
CROW	Countryside and Rights of Way Act, 2000.
CS	Chiltern Society
CWP	Chiltern Woodlands Project (from 1989 succeeding Small Woodlands Project)
DoE	Department of the Environment
DETR	Department of Environment, Transport and the Regions
DEFRA	Department of the Environment, Food and Rural Affairs
EC	Executive Council
FPC	Forward Planning Committee(s)
GR	Grid Reference
Group	Generally, a constituted Group of the Chiltern Society
HWBG,	Historic Works and Buildings Group (of the Chiltern Society)
LLA	London-Luton Airport
LADACAN	Luton and District Association for the Control of Airport Noise
MBE	Member of the British Empire
MSC	Manpower Services Commission
NCV	North Chilterns Volunteers
NRA	National Rivers Authority
OFWAT	Office of the Water Services Regulator
OS	Ordnance Survey
RAF	Royal Air Force
RDA	Regional Development Agency
RN	Royal Navy
ROWG	Rights of Way Group (of the Chiltern Society)
RWCG	Rivers and Wetlands Conservation Group (of the Chiltern Society)
SCCV	South Chilterns Conservation Volunteers, later the :
SCV	South Chiltern Volunteers (of the Chiltern Society)
SERPLAN	Sustainable Development Strategy for the South-East
SRA	Strategic Rail Authority
SUSTRANS	Sustainable Transport Ltd
SWOT	Strengths, Weaknesses, Opportunities and Threats (management exercise)
TWG	Trees and Woodlands Group (of the Chiltern Society)
TWIG	Trans-national Woodland Industries Group
WRG	Water Resources Group (of the Chiltern Society)